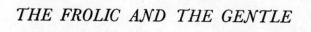

THE FROLIC AND THE GENTLE

CHARLES LAMB (AGED 51)

From the Painting by Henry Meyer in the India Office

The Frolic and the Gentle

A Centenary Study

of

CHARLES LAMB

by

A. C. Ward

KENNIKAT PRESS
Port Washington, N. Y./London

THE FROLIC AND THE GENTLE

First published in 1934
Reissued in 1970 by Kennikat Press
Library of Congress Catalog Card No: 78-103215
SBN 8046-0852-0

Manufactured by Taylor Publishing Company   Dallas, Texas

AUTHOR'S NOTE

CHARLES LAMB is not, I think, a suitable subject for psychological investigation, philosophical disquisition, or critical ingenuity. It seemed to me that the time had come for a short uncomplicated account of Lamb's experiences, friends and writings, and it is this I have sought to provide. As I proceeded with the book I became more and more aware that, on the biographical side, Mr. Lucas had left nothing new to be said, and hardly anything to be rediscovered. When I chanced to fish up some interesting piece of information from another source it almost invariably turned out to be already in E. V. Lucas's *Life of Lamb*, even when it had not been noted by the maker of his index. The only advantage I can claim over Mr. Lucas is that of brevity; his book is six times as long as mine. This means that I have been severely selective, whereas he was intentionally and invaluably exhaustive; and he remains for all time indispensable to the student of Lamb.

In the second part of the following study I have endeavoured to provide an independent analytical commentary upon Lamb's writings from the present-day standpoint. While this does not imply that I have approached him in an iconoclastic spirit, I have done whatever is possible to forget, temporarily, the fascination of the man and to consider him coolly as an author, isolating (as far as this is possible) his manner from his matter. And in dealing fairly fully with the non-Elian part of Lamb's work I may have uncovered for some readers a number of pieces in prose and verse that are in unmerited danger of being forgotten by all but a handful of enthusiasts.

A. C. WARD

CONTENTS

PROLOGUE

PAGE

THE GENIUS OF THE HEARTH 1

PART ONE: THE MAN

CHAPTER

I. CHILD AND SCHOOLBOY 17
II. CLERK AND BROTHER 38
III. THE FRIEND 54
IV. DOMESTICATION 76
V. BOOKS, PICTURES AND THE THEATRE . . 96
VI. THE LONDONER 106

PART TWO: THE WRITER

VII. CALENDAR OF WORKS 121
VIII. POET AND DRAMATIST 139
IX. *ROSAMUND GRAY*—CHILDREN'S BOOKS—
CRITICISM 158
X. *THE WORKS OF CHARLES LAMB*—UNCOL-
LECTED ESSAYS 176
XI. *ELIA* 190
XII. *THE LAST ESSAYS OF ELIA* 207

EPILOGUE

THE OLD ARMS OF HUMANITY 217

CHRONOLOGY 221

BIBLIOGRAPHY 223

INDEX 225

FRONTISPIECE

CHARLES LAMB (Aged 51)
By Henry Meyer, India Office.
(Reproduced by courtesy of the Under Secretary of State for India)

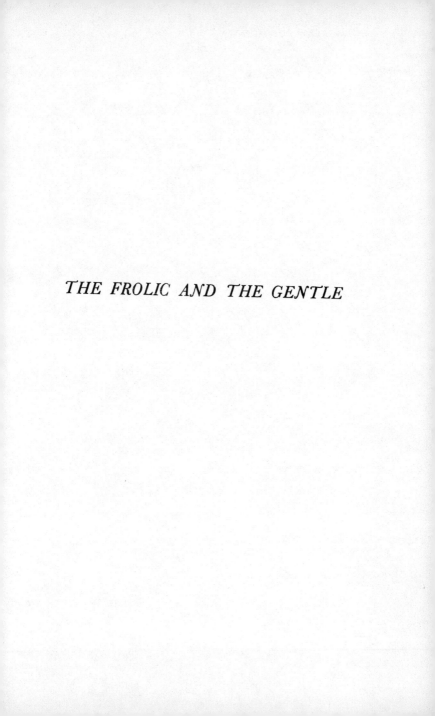

THE FROLIC AND THE GENTLE

PROLOGUE

THE GENIUS OF THE HEARTH

CHARLES LAMB was the Ordinary Man *in excelsis*, but this alone would not account for his extreme popularity at intervals during a hundred years. He also exactly conforms to the ordinary man's romantic idea of the Ordinary Man. The ordinary man is therefore able to see himself raised up and glorified in Lamb, and confirmed in the view that it is not the clever exceptional people who make the world go round, but the good and simple average people. And those of us who believe ourselves to be the Ordinary Man wish to be accounted good and simple before we are accounted clever. Charles Lamb's cleverness was a superfluity, a quality in him that might be subtracted without harm to the essential Lamb; or at least it is possible for us to think so. In the end, most of his readers do not value him so much for what he wrote as for what he was. They admit that they could not easily write like him (that, after all, was. where his "cleverness" came in), but they hope and believe they would behave in the crises of life as he behaved: it is proper for a man to behave so, and our average sympathies lie with what is proper, not with what is exceptional. There

B

is no other instance in literature of first-class writings being so dominated by the personality of the writer, and there is no other instance where it is impossible to consider the writings apart from the man. From the critical standpoint this is unfortunate, since it would appear almost traitorous to find fault (if one wished to find fault) with Lamb the author. It would seem that by so doing one was aspersing Lamb the brother, or Lamb the friend, or some other of those human Lambs who were so admirably unified in the man Charles. There is reason for believing that Lamb has never yet been critically valued as other authors have been, and it is probable that he never will be, on account of the manner in which he wove himself into his work. How is it possible to preserve a critical approach to (for instance) *Dream Children*, or *Old China*, or *The Superannuated Man*? All these, and most of *Elia*, are so supercharged with personal feeling that the reader either succumbs at once to the sentiment and thereby disables his critical faculty, or he dislikes the supercharge so intensely that his bile rises and unfits him for any steady intellectual examination. This has not only prevented a coolly critical attitude in regard to Lamb himself, but it has also made a majority of readers incapable of approaching his contemporary essayists fairly. After a term on the warm hearthstone of Elia, a chill falls when Hazlitt is opened. Yet was not Hazlitt's the finer intelligence and the more cultivated taste? The fact that the mere asking of this question sounds heretical and a little indecent affords a measure of the extent to which we have become content to glow warmly in the companionable presence of Elia. He stands alone in literature and we will not suffer comparisons because he contrived to unite the pattern of commonplace virtue with genius in presentation. As Lamb apparently was, so the larger part of mankind wishes to see itself: kindly, self-sacrificing, tenacious, whimsical, companionable, domesticated, with just that lightly-borne bookishness which stops short on this side of pedantry. It would not, assuredly, diminish Lamb's standing and reputation if his world should be taken to represent the apotheosis of the commonplace. Literature that is academically approved has, on the whole, lived too much by qualities of the head and insufficiently by those of the blood. By so doing, literature has often deliberately avoided its most exacting tasks, those which demand the finest and most delicate exercise of literary discipline. The mind is the docile part of man, the heart is intractable. If the need to discipline emotion were not the major difficulty of authorship an Ella Wheeler Wilcox might become another Shakespeare, for the basic emotions of any sweet singer from Wisconsin are identical with those of the greatest poets: it is in the factor of control that they differ vastly. On his own plane, Lamb's emotional discipline is perfect. We may be temperamentally averse from the public show of warm emotion, but we cannot question his ability to keep it within bounds.

Lamb's genius was that of the hearth, not of the heights, and the hearth is conducive neither to profound thought nor to tempestuous feeling. Lamb could hold his own with such greater men as Wordsworth and Coleridge, but he did so more by the play of a ready wit and native commonsense than by equivalence of intellectual power and metaphysical penetration. It was perhaps because channels of experience wide open to them were closed to him that Lamb appears to us to have been much saner than they were. He kept to the levels of common experience, and being insulated from their possibilities of exaltation he was safeguarded also from the occasional ponderous bathos of Wordsworth as well as from Coleridge's tendency to be, at moments, either fretfully petty or ludicrously abstracted. Someone has said that Lamb was in the world but not of it, but that saying is only doubtfully accurate. It suggests that Lamb was withdrawn from the world and immersed in himself, and nothing could be less in accordance with the facts. If a frequent use of the letter "I" is a guarantee of egoism, then Lamb was an egoist. He himself made that allegation against himself, yet he was as far from any trace of megalomania as it is humanly possible to be. A friend's impression was that "Charles Lamb seemed not for a moment to rest on self, but to throw his whole soul into the nature of circumstances and things around him." Incapable though we may be of a critical attitude toward him, he himself did not share that incapacity. Because he was so fully alive to the world immediately about him, he saw himself as part of that world, not himself as its hub. His lively sense of the absurd was one of the things he shared with the Ordinary Man. He had no wish to be a remarkable character; he preferred to merge into his surroundings, to be an insignificant figure in unnoticeable shabby clothes. A well-known apocryphal story, supposed to have been told by Lamb, serves as a parable of the innate difference between him and the other-worldliness of Coleridge. He declared that one morning while walking to the office he met Coleridge, who drew him aside into a sheltered corner, took him by the button of the coat and, with closed eyes, began a prolonged monologue. "I listened entranced", Lamb said; "but the striking of a church-clock recalled me to a sense of duty. I saw it was of no use to attempt to break away, so taking advantage of his absorption in his subject, I, with my penknife, quietly severed the button from my coat and decamped. Five hours afterwards, in passing the same garden, on my way home, I heard Coleridge's voice, and on looking in, there he was, with closed eyes,—the button in his fingers,—and his right hand gracefully waving, just as when I left him. He had never missed me." The virtual certainty that the incident never happened is of no importance, for if Lamb invented it there is all the more reason for noting that his way with philosophers and philosophy was to sever himself from them and go about his business. Duty and the common world took hold of his mind to the exclusion of speculation and imaginative flights. He would suffer philosophers gladly but he would not be taken-in by them. The Ordinary Man therefore receives from Lamb the comforting impression that there was no humbug about him, and the impression is correct. He may not have been able to look deeply into the mind of the universe or profoundly into the nature of things, but he could see clearly into the hearts of people. And that, thinks the Ordinary Man, should be the principal concern of men and women.

§ 2

Would Lamb's intermittent popularity have been as remarkable as it has been if we did not know that he was "unfortunate" and one of the leading characters in a painful domestic tragedy? It is scarcely necessary to attempt to answer the question, because it is short-circuited in advance by our inability to think of a successful Lamb, burgeoning with prosperity and satisfaction. The world does not, despite the popular jingle, laugh with the laughers and turn its back upon the weepers. Quite contrary to this notion, it delights to suck melancholy from the woes of others, provided always that the woeful bear up bravely and wear their willow with a bright flourish. We love to think of ourselves as the sport of destiny, bowed but not broken by unmerited wrongs. We do, in fact, if we are introspective at all—and who is not?—think of ourselves continuously in that semblance. Our unjust and oppressive destiny may take the form of a daily occupation that is drudging and tiresome, but it serves us as a personal version of the spectacle of a strong man (or a noble woman) struggling with Fate. And having no Greek tragedy within sight and sound to purge us with pity and terror arising from a contemplation of the afflictions of others—or, rather, not dramatising ourselves as heroic figures in conflict with principalities and powers—we find comfort and upliftment in taking to our hearts some such domestic tragedy as Lamb's. We think it highly improbable that anything of the sort will happen to us; we pray that it may not; but that need not hinder us from experiencing a vicarious nobility. By an effort we might perchance imagine Lamb as a happy husband and father, writing equally charming essays on other subjects than those with which circumstance actually provided him; but if we do this, it is more than our faculties will stretch to to imagine that we should be, in the changed conditions, as interested in and attracted by Lamb as we now are after the lapse of a century. Take away Mary Lamb and the emotional significance she has for us in relation to her brother's life and work, and a large part of Charles' power over posterity would vanish. Wordsworth had a sister, to whom he addressed some lovely poems. Dorothy Wordsworth was as devoted to William as Mary Lamb was to Charles, and she had a greater influence on his writings; but posterity has shown only a limited human interest in William and Dorothy. There was no tragedy—none, that is, of a dramatisable sort— though we may wonder whether there was not as much distress of another kind in Dorothy Wordsworth's life as in Mary Lamb's. The world cannot be said to have a literary interest in Charles Lamb; it has a human affection for him. His audience must be very much larger than that which waits upon any other author of his sort, except (possibly) Robert Louis Stevenson, whose case in on a par with that of Lamb. Many fewer people would read Stevenson as an essayist if he had not also been "unfortunate" and as courageous about his misfortune as Lamb was about his own different one. Yet courage, in this connection, is not enough. No one achieves popularity by laughing off his troubles. It is necessary to tinge one's fortitude with a trifle of romantic melancholy; one's pen must suggest a pathetic catch of the breath from time to time; one must smile so that one shall not weep. The thing can now be done to a precise formula, but there was no formula for Lamb to follow. He originated it—not as a formula, however. He felt before he wrote, and wrote no more than the feeling spontaneously prompted him to write. He triumphs not by the formula, but by the sincerity behind the formula. Nevertheless, there is a formula. Lamb was too good an artist to depend upon hazard, and a formula, carefully calculated, was essential if writing so heavily charged with emotion was to be saved from collapsing into a sentimental morass. The nature of the Elia formula is discussed elsewhere in this book, and it is unnecessary to say more here on this topic; though, for the avoidance of further confusion in a direction where a vast confusion already exists, it is desirable to add a little on the matter of sincerity in writing such as Lamb's. There are readers, there must be thousands of them, who suppose that sincerity and spontaneity are inseparable in literature, especially when it is of the closely personal sort. If sentences intended to have an emotional effect are subjected to a process of deliberate shaping and refining, these people hold that sincerity disappears as artifice comes in. The reverse is true. There are two kinds of sincerity to be considered when the literary rendering of emotion is under discussion. So far as the internal evidence in her work is to be taken into account, there is no reason to think that Miss Wilhelmina Stitch's verses are other than sincerely conceived and spontaneously expressed. But some readers would unhesitatingly say that while the authoress may be in the human sense entirely sincere, her work in the technical sense is insincere. She does not, we may well believe, say more than she means, nor say it more emphatically than she genuinely desires. The critical objection that might be made is on the ground that she does say more than the quality of the emotion warrants, that she says it more emphatically than the quality warrants, and that the quality of the expression is inappropriate to its circumstance in print—that, in other words, there is an absence of precision and reticence. Genius is a law unto itself, yet it is improbable that geniuses find precision and reticence going hand in hand with spontaneity. The human impulse is to "write as one feels", knowing that it is natural to speak as one feels. But the sincerity of speech is different from the sincerity of writing. Speech is, properly, spontaneous; writing is, inevitably, deliberate. A sincere person speaks as he feels *at the moment*; what he says is a temporary statement. Literature, to be sincere, should aim at saying, so far as such things can be calculated, not simply what is felt at the moment but what will also be felt tomorrow and for ever. That is why we can still, in the very different mood of this century, read without a blush the powerfully emotional essays of Elia written early last century. He expresses the permanent state of emotions, not their passing superflux. Well might he say, though playfully, that he would write for antiquity. Antiquity would have responded to his rendering of emotion as aptly as posterity does. What would *Dream Children* have been like if written with spontaneous gusto by an author who "wrote as he felt"? We cannot bear to think of it. As Lamb left it, *Dream Children* is marvellously poised between reticence and intense feeling. It is never permitted to use one uncalculated word that would destroy the poise, and at the same time there is no trace of niggardliness in the use of emotion. It never refrains from saying enough, though it always avoids saying more than enough. Finding this exact poise is the whole art of emotional writing. Anyone who has ever written spontaneously under the immediate stress of powerful feeling, knows what uncomfortable sensations such writing stirs when it is re-read by the writer after an interval. The only exception to this is when a practised writer has learned to discipline (and therefore to diminish the stress of) feeling at the moment of writing, out of the knowledge (born from experience) that what he feels today he will not feel with the same force tomorrow or next week. The principal reason for exercising such discipline and reticence is that a mere gush of emotion will not stir a corresponding emotion in a perceptive reader. Readers are much more in the position of the writer's tomorrow's self; they are not fired with unbridled emotion and they are suspicious or resentful of what appears to be over-statement. "Sincere" writing is that which represents with fitting reticence the permanencies of emotion, and avoids its temporary excesses.

§ 3

Will Charles Lamb hold his place as one of the "masters" of English literature? No certain answer can be given, whether that question is asked about Lamb or anyone else. If it be asked whether there is absolute merit in his work, there need be less hesitancy in giving a confident reply. Every absolute merit has its relative aspect, however, and is at any given time rated high or low according to the fluctuations of contemporary taste and opinion. The thermometer of Lamb's reputation has been subject to a full share of these vagaries, and it probably reached its maximum height in the early years of the twentieth-century, by which time the wave of nineteenth-century romanticism had spread to every section of the literate and semi-literate population. Thanks (if *thanks* is the right word) to popular education, practically everyone in the English-speaking world had learned to read, and a gradually increasing Liberal tradition, with its romantic doctrine of humane tolerance, had produced an enormously large audience of the type that could and did appreciate Lamb. From 1900 to 1914 was the modern golden age of tolerance and enlightenment, or so it seems now that bigotry and obscurantism are once more in the ascendant. Hardly anyone could have been found in England during that period to question the supremacy of Lamb among those writers who have exploited the "familiar style". Lamb's only possible rival was Robert Louis Stevenson, who was cherished by the many for exactly similar qualities. Now the stock of both these essayists has slumped considerably, and it will help to put Lamb in proper perspective if some of the reasons for this temporary decline in popularity can be isolated, noting by the way, as a fact of special importance, that it is only among the *intelligentsia* that he is less esteemed than he was in the first decade and a half of this century. The varying fortunes of Lamb's reputation depend quite as much upon social change as upon any simply literary standard of judgment. Indeed, notwithstanding his reputed bookishness, Lamb is one of the least literary figures in literature, and his fame is much more susceptible to human factors than to intellectual ones. Round about the nineteen-tens the immense earnestness of nineteenth-century England had fallen to low ebb, and it was scarcely possible for anyone to take the bitterly contemptuous view of Lamb that Carlyle had taken. It is reasonable to go further and say that the mood of Elia exactly coincided for a stretch of years with the temper of the new Edwardian England. He, like it, was tentative, humane, undogmatic, susceptible to the gentler emotions, and endlessly hospitable to the large uncritical simplicities of life. The heart ruled the head in Edward VII's England, as Lamb's head was ruled by his heart. Moreover, pre-War England still believed in the home as the centre of things and it still believed in the importance and permanence of human relationships. It was an England that now seems incredible even to those who lived and grew up in it. In those days anyone who read at all read the *Essays of Elia* as a matter of course; and, as a matter of course, one included them among "the classics" even if (as rarely happened) one did not quite see what the fuss and enthusiasm were about. In the nineteen-thirties all that has changed. The surviving Edwardians find themselves absent-mindedly assuming that Lamb still stands where he did when they were young and ingenuous, and it is only by keeping their wits about them that they are able to remember that now, to some of the Georgians and most of the post-Georgians, Lamb is definitely out of the picture. Amid the roar of centenary plaudits a continuous thin piping of shrill dissent is certain to be heard, and Mr. L. will be damned afresh with hisses. Yet this will have nothing whatsoever to do with Lamb and his true reputation. If the present generation thinks less of Lamb than its fathers and aunts did, it is only because, according to current belief, the large, simple, humane, urbane and tolerant view of life has been "found out". The English home has dwindled to the rank of a *caravanserai*, lifelong affections have been replaced by week-end passions, familiar conversation has been drowned by the simultaneity of endless dogmatic monologues which no one heeds because everyone is monologising. Lamb has not changed, but those who would in the normal

course have formed his willing and quiet audience
have changed. Possibly he never again will have an
audience so much in tune with him as that 1900–1914
assembly was. Victorian moral cocksureness had gone;
post-War intellectual arrogance had not been born.
The world was—for a final hour—quiet; ominously
quiet as we now know. English men and women still
believed in doing their duty, as Lamb did his; but
though it was the obvious thing to do they, like him,
disliked behaving solemnly about it. They believed
in fidelity and human solidarity, instead of in promis-
cuity and class- or party-consciousness. This was the
soil in which Elia could flourish as he did not flourish
in his own lifetime, and as he cannot flourish in the
present or in the near future, if a large proportion of
readers is to be regarded as having permanently "gone
intellectual". Intellectualists may find in Elia esoteric
significances not yet divulged to the larger and popular
audience; they may acclaim him afresh and establish
for him a new reputation based upon such merits as
Lamb himself would not have set much store by. As
these words are being written, a leader of one of the
groups of advanced modernist writers is commending
a "Laboratory of the Mystic Logos", in which dying
literary forms are to be finally annihilated, making
way for new creations in a primitive grammar—a
"stammering that approaches the language of God".
Before I read that manifesto I had written (Chapter XI
in this book) of Lamb's divine stammer in the style
of Elia. It may be that Lamb's reputation will become
re-established as the prophet of the Laboratory of the
Mystic Logos. He certainly knew a great deal about
the art and business of writing; some of the things
he knew and either took for granted or ignored have

been held up before the post-War generation as original discoveries made by the Modernists themselves. But Lamb knew it all, and could have taught our innovators a good deal they went further afield for—to Proust and other exotic sources. First and last, however, though the "mystic logos" and its power was not hidden from him, nor hidden by him from others, Lamb depended largely upon other sources of power which are not shut away in any portentous intellectualist laboratory.

PART ONE
THE MAN

CHAPTER ONE

CHILD AND SCHOOLBOY

§ 1

THE London into which Charles Lamb was born on February 10, 1775, was a city of character as well as a haunt of characters. If the streets were narrower, darker and dirtier than those trodden by its twentieth-century inhabitants, they were not blighted by the scabrous patches of settled squalor which now lie behind the magnificent frontages of wholesale commerce and retail trade. London's dirt was then nearer to honest natural dirt; the city's pauperism, in Lamb's words, was old and honourable; and from both dirt and pauperism the Londoner could escape outside the city gates into the pleasant pastures of villages that have since become absorbed and modernized into slums—Islington, Hoxton, Dalston, Shacklewell, Hackney: Beggars and mendicants too have gone; unemployment exchanges have ousted them. From end to end, the metropolis is regimented, and not half-a-dozen queer characters remain to be seen in a week's perambulation of the highways and byways of what is no longer a city but —imponderable monster—an administrative county thronged by millions having votes but no proud sense of citizenship.

We cannot easily get into imaginative touch with Lamb unless we somehow acclimatise our senses to his environment, stranger to us than China or Cathay. Men are merely men nowadays; and shops merely shops, except when they are department stores. In Lamb's day, men were distinguishable one from another by the profession they followed or the craft they plied. A scrivener would not be mistaken for a lawyer, nor an author for a butcher; there were, recognisable to the wayfarer, pretty milliners and neat seamstresses—now these are all alike machinists in name and mere women and girls in appearance. The contents of any Pentonville omnibus might be emptied into Bond Street or into Whitechapel and appear completely and indifferently at home in either place. Pastry-cooks' and silversmiths' are faded into shops simply—their individuality gone. Where, formerly, tea-sellers scooped out their aromatic rustling leaves from bins and weighed their ounces with a flourish of bright scales held at eye-level, preparatory to wrapping the tea with proud skill that no layman could imitate, the grocer now reaches down a packet identical with the packets supplied to 197,000 shops throughout the kingdom. These changes may be for our good, but they are changes so substantial that in total they amount to the coming of a different world. Lamb lived in a London where exceptions were the rule and oddity of manner the custom. In our London, to be either odd or exceptional is tantamount to an offence against law and order. Most of the assertions that Dickens was mainly a caricaturist ignore the effect industrialism has had upon civilised character. In a handmade world, men and women were dif-ferentiated as patently as were the products of their hands; differentiation was the mode. The precision of the machine, turning out endless supplies of identical articles, has in our day made indistinguishable identity the fashion even for human beings. By the wisdom of God, our faces were made different one from another, but the modern manner has decreed that this was simply an unfortunate whim of the deity, and one to be corrected by artifice in the beauty parlour or in less secluded spots. We have forsaken individuality and sunk dully upon uniformity. Lamb, if he could re-visit the world, would be unendurable to any who are indisposed to approve the widest and sharpest differences between one human being and another. Too much of the extravagant adulation of Lamb is apologetic in character: that is to say, it depends upon exaggeration of the qualities in him that we individually admire and upon diminution of those we dislike. But, to be honest, we must take Charles Lamb in the whole piece. He would have been the last to wish to be taken by posterity in any other way, for he was the implacable enemy of humbug whether toward the living or the dead. To be acclaimed on false pretences, to be approved in any other manner than with all his faults upon him—this he would have considered to be the most heinous of posthumous insults. As men go, his faults were few enough to absolve us from any dutiful feeling that we ought to labour to make them appear fewer. Even if it could be proved that in his *Confessions of a Drunkard* he was painting a direct self-portrait, it would be unpardonable in us to seek to excuse him or to explain away the circumstances. A man should be judged by the positive merit of his good deeds—if, indeed, it is any part of our business to proceed to judgment at all. We know well what Charles Lamb's positive virtues were; they stand secure against whatever weaknesses he may also have had, and they would not be lessened by any statistics of alcoholic excess that biographical ingenuity might adduce. The one obligation that does rest upon us is to take the man as he was, perhaps like ourselves in much; possibly better than we are in the simple-hearted consistency of his devotion to one whom he might have been excused for committing to the care of others; worse than we are, maybe, in his inability to overcome indulgences—too much drink and tobacco—that harassed him constantly. But the balance-sheet of his life shows him to have been as admirable a specimen of mankind as history has to show. The probability remains, however, that if we could be transported to one of his famous weekly parties we should "like" him less in his habit as he lived than we do at a distance in the pages of *Elia*, where his oddity is united with a picturesque quaintness and his boisterousness with whimsicality.

§ 2

We could conveniently manage with less information than we actually have concerning some phases of Charles Lamb's life, but our knowledge of his childhood is regrettably sparse. John Lamb, Charles' father, came from Lincolnshire stock and married Elizabeth Field whose family belonged to Hertfordshire, the place which, next to London, is most closely connected with the names of Charles and Mary his sister. These two, with the eldest brother John, were all that survived childhood out of a family of seven, the first of whom was born in 1762, when the father was about thirty-seven. Charles, the youngest, was born at 2 Crown Office Row in the Temple, where his father was clerk and resident factotum to one of the benchers of the Inner Temple, Samuel Salt. Both obliquely and directly John Lamb appears a number of times in his son's writings, and we gather that as a small boy he came up to London from Lincolnshire to go into service, being duly wept over by his mother at their parting. Of John's progress in the metropolis we know nothing, but from his own volume of light verse, *Poetical Pieces on Several Occasions*, it is evident that he was at one time living in Bath and that he had been a footman. According to Charles' account John Lamb was, in his prime, a cheerful little man resembling Garrick in countenance, and addicted to a variety of pastimes —fishing, modelling in clay and plaster, woodworking, card-playing and punch-mixing, as well as versifying. He was also fastidiously honest and loyal, sometimes to his personal disadvantage, having on one occasion put aside the opportunity of a lucrative post in the Treasury of the Temple by pleading the cause of the offending occupant, who would have been discharged but for John Lamb's intervention. Unhappily, as Charles grew up, the father's faculties waned and grief made him at length a broken man and a sore burden; but, as we see him in the earlier and more flourishing days, he belonged to that now almost extinct type of retainer who is half servant, half companion, combining the two functions without either obsequiousness or presumption.

Under normal conditions it is likely that at least as much would have been known about Mrs. Lamb, but, for reasons which will appear later, scarcely anything was written about her. It was, however, to their maternal grandmother, Mary Field, that the young Lambs went visiting in Hertfordshire, storing their memories unconsciously with material that was afterwards to flow with natural ease on to many of their written pages. But before the Hertfordshire holidays are touched upon more fully, there is the family circle in the Temple to consider. Of the six persons comprising it, all but Charles and Mary (who was eleven years older) are shadowy figures of varying degrees of tenuity.

Of the elders in the circle the one who has been made to appear most substantial was John Lamb's sister, Sarah, called by the children aunt Hetty. She was both tearful and devout, and being "one whom single blessedness had soured to the world" Sarah was inclined to consider herself denied a proper meed of attention in the household. Her affections concentrated upon Charles almost exclusively, though her queer mannerisms of staring beneath her spectacles and mumbling were a source of fear to the child. At such times she appeared as a grotesque to him, and this, combined with imaginings started by Foxe's *Book of Martyrs*, a history of witches, and sundry lurid pictures out of a biblical history, caused young Charles to become terrified lest aunt Hetty should turn out to belong to the frightful witches' brood. This in turn gave rise to nervous horrors that made the solitary night-time a recurrent hell for the boy. But Sarah Lamb was, in truth, ill-cast for the part of an authentic witch. She was kindness embodied when dealing with her favourite nephew, cooking him good things to eke out the summary fare to which he would otherwise have been confined while at school. In matters of religion, aunt Hetty was assiduous without narrowness. She read Thomas à Kempis and a Roman Catholic prayer-book, but went to church a good Protestant every Sunday, only turning aside from the Establishment for a period to attend the Unitarian chapel in Essex Street, Strand, into which she had wandered curiously one day, remaining to discover that she liked the sermon and the form of service. When, years later, Charles Lamb belaboured the writers of namby-pamby children's books and regretted the passing of "that beautiful interest in wild tales which made the child a man, while all the time he suspected himself to be no bigger than a child", he may well have been thinking of the days in which he was, quite likely, fed upon tales and old wives' fables by aunt Hetty.

From two casual references in the essays there is reason to suppose that Charles was attacked by small-pox when he was five, and that at some time in his childhood he was unable to walk far because of lameness and had to be carried many a mile by his brother John, who was senior by twelve years. He must therefore be thought of as a somewhat delicate as well as a sensitive and highly imaginative boy, and it is probable that his first visit with Mary to the Hertfordshire grandmother was dictated as much by physical necessity as by the desire to cure his distressful and persistent night-fears. Mrs. Field at that time was in charge of an untenanted mansion at Blakesware, in Hertfordshire. She had been in service with the Plumer family for many years and (in the absence of members of the family, who owned another estate in the county) was in sole occupation of Blakesware from 1778 until she died in 1792. Lamb adorns the facts somewhat in his own account of the place and his visit thereto, but it may be taken that his recollections of Mary Field are substantially accurate. She was tall, upright and graceful until cancer misshaped her body but left her spirit untouched. The boy rambled alone about the great house, in and out of its bare echoing rooms, in which tapestries and threadbare hangings fluttered in the draughts that swept through the vast and for-saken apartments. Out of doors were spacious grounds still tended by a gardener who kept watch over the nectarines and peaches; and there—in the orangery, or among the yews and firs, or beside the fish-pool at the end of the garden—young Charles recovered his nerve and thereafter, no doubt, owed more to the country than, faithful Londoner as he was, he was ready to allow. But his earliest memories were not of Blakesware. While still in weakling infancy he was taken by Mary Lamb to stay with his other Hertfordshire relations, the Gladmans, who lived in a farmhouse at Mackery End, between Wheathamp-stead and Harpenden; Charles's recollections of this visit were too faint to be detailed without aid in his essay-writing days, and it was an excursion some decades later that provided the material for the Mackery End paper by Elia. Mary however was in her teens at the earlier time, and it is assumed that Louisa Manners' story in *Mrs. Leicester's School* is an account, only faintly disguised, of their stay at the farm. The young people saw everything pertaining to the farmer's daily round, and, except bird-nesting, nothing much was forbidden them. They sat up late to watch the sheep-shearing supper, when the com-pany gathered round a long carved oak table, mirror bright. And being at last sent upstairs (while the festivities were still vigorous) they lay in bed listening to the songs, very loud and very fine, though they could not make out the words. But so far as Charles is concerned it was Blakesware, not Mackery End, that caused Hertfordshire to be encircled in his mind with a halo of old romance. Grandmother Field had a spartan way with children, never hesitating to submit them to drastic handling for what she thought to be their good. She evidently had small sympathy for the reserved and solitary young pair who, Charles especially, found a strange satisfaction in brooding about the great place. The elder brother, John Lamb, was her favourite; he was a handsome and spirited youth who rode and sought the company of the hunters, bringing something of the bustle of the larger outside world into the life of the old lady who, no doubt, had solitude enough in her guardianship of the lonely house and was disinclined to spare patience for the silent little figure that stole, a trifle uncannily, about the rooms and passages, sometimes standing for hours in the deserted hall staring at the busts of the Roman emperors ranged about the walls. Nevertheless, Lamb had few other than loving and grateful thoughts for grandmother Field. She and the husk of a house she reigned over occasioned some of the best pages her then unpromising nephew was ever to write, and this would not have been so if there had been no more to say than that her mercies were cruel ones.

§ 3

Biographical tradition usually preserves some youthful saying to demonstrate that the future eminence of notable people was foreshadowed in childhood: the younger Nelson is reported to have been as great a stranger to fear as Washington was to lying. The bland irony which was to be a characteristic feature in Charles Lamb's mature essays is rarely to be found lurking, even in embryo, in the child mind, but hearsay preserved one anecdote which Lamb's first biographer, Serjeant Talfourd, recorded as evidence that the small boy had, in however crude a form, some trace of the subtle penetration which afterwards moved him to pull aside the veil of gush and pretence wherever he detected its presence. He and Mary were lingering in a churchyard one day when he was very young, deciphering the inscriptions on the tombstones. Charles was plainly impressed by the tributes to the uniform goodness of the buried, but, noting the sharp difference between this parade of virtue and what he had already observed of the behaviour of the living, he inquired, "Mary, where are the naughty people buried?" This challenging directness must, in fact, have been a part of Lamb's natural make-up, for it is supported by his sharp and critical remembrances of those who were his earliest teachers at school.

In succession to whatever he had learned informally through companionship with Mary, Lamb took his first formal lessons from a Mrs. Reynolds, to whom he was ever afterwards devoted. When she was old and indigent he settled upon her a pension of some £30 a year, and visitors to the Lamb household would meet this strange elderly woman, who could have given him no more than the barest elements of learning. But Mrs. Reynolds had another claim to distinction. She had known Oliver Goldsmith, and was permitted to borrow his copy of *The Deserted Village*. This link with the great literary circle of the eighteenth century serves to remind us that Charles Lamb was born in the twilight of the Johnsonian era. Dr. Johnson died when Lamb was eight, and it is not inconceivable that the lad may have encountered the shambling bulk of the old literary lawgiver during their mutual peram- bulations of Fleet Street, a thoroughfare to which Lamb's affection was very specially given. But even if he never walked in Johnson's shadow, he came into close touch with one who must have been a rather Johnsonian person—William Bird, the keeper of an academy that overlooked a drab garden in a passage running from Fetter Lane to Bartlett's Buildings. There, Lamb first went to school, and in his adult recollection Bird was an awesome memory—squat, corpulent, middle-sized, wearing an Indian gown so strangely patterned that the children believed it to be covered with hieroglyphics of an unknown but sinister significance. The academy purported to pro- vide tuition in writing, languages and mathematics, and Lamb supposed that Bird was, on the whole, a humane and judicious mentor, despite his addiction to a ferocious instrument of correction, the blister- raiser, resembling a heavy wooden spoon with a large hole carved in the bowl. This brought up blisters on the hands of the delinquent pupils to whom the weapon was forcefully applied. Packed so tightly amid his desk-companions that "free-hand" writing was physically impossible, Lamb attributed his rather cramped script to that cause; yet at the age of fifty he still looked back with gratified vanity upon his achievement in winning the prize for spelling at William Bird's school. As uncertainty about spelling was a congenital failing with Charles Lamb, and one he never surmounted, the carrying-off of this award must be accounted as one of those happy academic mysteries which beset most people at some point in their educational careerings.

Mary, Mrs. Reynolds and Bird prepared the way for the boy's entrance to Christ's Hospital in the autumn of 1782. Mr. Lamb's employer, Samuel Salt, is commonly supposed to have been mainly instrumental in securing Charles' admission, though the actual guarantor for his good behaviour was Timothy Yeats. That Samuel Salt was in fact the prime mover is plain from Lamb's own statement that he was insured against severity or tyranny while at the school because it was known that his patron "lived in a manner under his (the boy's) paternal roof"—a typical instance of Lamb's sly humour, seeing that it was they who lived under the patron's roof in the Temple. The Blue-coat school at that time stood in Newgate Street (on the site of the present General Post Office) with the grim bulk of Newgate Prison—just then rebuilt with a discouraging ornamentation of fetters—confronting it across the road, a vaster and more horrific version of the dungeons which lay in wait for offenders within the precincts of the school. In his first essay on Christ's Hospital Lamb painted an almost elysian picture of school life. Subsequently, in the Elia essay, he touched it in with darker tones, avoiding the appearance of inconsistency by representing the school partly through the eyes of Coleridge, who entered at the same time as Lamb and remained two years longer. There seems no doubt that Coleridge was more tenderly sensitive than his companion and that, being out of touch with his family, he had no such compensations as Lamb enjoyed in the way of consolatory visits and supplementary repasts. Both witnesses give almost identical descriptions of the daily meals, the unappetising meagreness of which is plain enough. But from the Temple to Newgate was a journey that elderly aunt Hetty could manage with fair ease, and —half eagerly, half shamefacedly—Charles would welcome her frequent arrivals with some appetising morsel she had abstracted for him from the family table. He has described how she would come and sit upon the coal-hole steps with a basin wrapped in her apron, himself too hungry to consider overmuch the other ravenous youngsters who stood by, watchful but unregarded, in the cloisters. The numerous holidays gave opportunity in the summer for delicious excursions to the New River, which ran not far distant from the school. In winter, too, such times of release were welcomed by Lamb, who could then satisfy his home-seeking proclivities; but, to Coleridge, there was no equivalent solace—only the dark friendless streets to wander through without purpose, or the gloomy Tower to visit again and again for want of a happier haunt: there at least were the familiar faces of the Beefeaters and the hope of a cheery word from those picturesque janitors, who had orders to admit the Blue-coat boys whenever they presented themselves. Still looking at his old school as it were from Coleridge's point of view, Lamb speaks of the severity of the masters (though one, as we know from a following passage, was all too lenient) and, especially, of the monitors' tyrannical treatment of the younger boys, whom they thrashed savagely with leathern thongs, and drove from the fire in the depth of winter; while the school nurses, to add to the tale of hardships, regularly purloined considerable portions of the few eatable meals served up to the juniors. Lamb first wrote about Christ's Hospital to defend it against the charges of those who alleged that it had been diverted from the purpose of its original foundation (in 1552) by Edward VI, who laid it down that the school should take under its fostering care the fatherless and other poor children. After two hundred years and more there was no longer, so Lamb argued, the same need to confine the Christ's scholars to those most needy classes, who were by that time amply provided for by other generous agencies. In changed circumstances the Governors of Christ's Hospital felt free to take a proportion of the sons of respectable parents whose limited resources did not permit them to give their children a fitting education. It is difficult not to regard this as a piece of dubious special pleading, yet it is mitigated by the touching story told by Elia of the cross-eyed boy who became a sort of pariah in the school because of his inexplicable habit of gathering-up the scraps of food rejected at table by the others. These he used to store in the chest beside his bed, though he was never discovered to eat them. As, on leave days, he had been observed carrying away something wrapped in a large blue handkerchief, it was supposed that he sold the scraps to beggars, and he was sent to coventry by the school. But the detective instinct of boys will out, and at length the culprit was followed to a tumble-down apartment in Chancery Lane, whither he carried his unsavoury bundle. The recipients of the leavings were found to be the boy's hungry parents and, the story becoming known, the Governors of the school voted the family an allowance and gave the child a silver medal, the presentation of this providing the fit opportunity for a lesson on the evils of rash judgment. The sequel to this story, while supplying evidence that Christ's Hospital was still fulfilling its function in relation to the very poor, at the same time supports in a measure Lamb's contention that the lowest classes should be given only such instruction as may be beneficial and not pernicious to them. The hero of the scrap-gathering episode was afterwards seen by Lamb carrying a baker's basket, and, as he apparently did no good for himself later on, the advantages of a classical education were not apparent in his case.

The dungeons of the school, where runaways (in particular) suffered solitary confinement, were "little, square, Bedlam cells, where a boy could just lie at length upon straw and a blanket . . . with a peep of light, let in askance, from a prison orifice at top, barely enough to read by". This form of punishment was abandoned after it had driven one or two unfortunates either out of their senses or to attempt suicide, and its institution provoked Lamb to one of his few bitter utterances: he declared that he would willingly spit upon the statue of Howard, who was responsible for the dungeon torments. These things and the scarifying ritual in hall which attended the expulsion of third-offenders represented the darker side of the Bluecoats' life, and Lamb spoke reluctantly upon such topics, since his chief recollections were of happier matters. The masters, Rev. Matthew Field and Rev. James Boyer, gave him scope for two of his best character-sketches. Field and Boyer conducted their classics classes simultaneously in one room. The former, Lamb's master in the Lower School, spent his time principally away from his scholars, and often entirely away from the school, while the class, left to its own ingenuities, passed the hours in "mirth and uproar", in reading adventure stories (*Peter Wilkins* and the like), or in making cat-cradles and paper sundials. Meanwhile, on the other side of the imaginary line which was all that separated the two classes, the Upper School would be sweating over Xenophon and Plato, themselves silent beside the contiguous uproar and doubly shaken when Boyer (unconcerned by his colleague's neglected rabble) roared at the ignorance or imagined insolence of his own myrmidons. Coleridge, who was under Boyer, ranked him highly as a teacher, and at Boyer's death (referring to his birching proclivities) made one of the very neatest of his rare jokes: "Poor J.B.!—may all his faults be forgiven; and may he be wafted to bliss by little cherub boys, all head and wings, with no *bottoms* to reproach his sublunary infirmities." Lamb records this remark, which in its peculiar kind sounds too good for Coleridge and good enough for the recorder himself.

During his seven years as a Blue-coat boy Lamb progressed to the rank of a Deputy-Grecian. The Grecians were the exalted seniors of the school, very few in number and destined for the university and the Church. Lamb had a pronounced impediment in his speech which made a clerical career out of the question—as it was inappropriate also on other grounds —and he did not, therefore, enter the select fold of the Grecians. In after life he counted the influence of the Christ's Hospital tradition as one of the most plainly manifest benefits conferred by the school upon those who had experienced its nurture. It imparted dignity and composure, pride and modesty, confidence and reserve. He wrote, in 1813, that the scholars refrained from eating the fat of certain boiled meats, as a kind of ceremonial self-denial—discipline extended also to some sorts of sweet cake. But in 1820 he attributed this rejection of fat to what was most probably its true cause—that "children are universally fat-haters". The difference in temper as between the two Christ's Hospital papers is extremely interesting to students of Lamb. Apart from the circumstance that the earlier essay was in some degree an *apologia* for the policy of the Governors, a good deal has to be allowed for the greater sense of freedom he obviously experienced when writing under the Elia pseudonym. That he felt tenderly for his school there can be no doubt, and any attack upon it would be certain to stir him to a chivalrous defence. Possibly, after the first essay appeared, Coleridge and other friends who had also been to Christ's criticised his uniformly roseate account. Whatever the reason, whereas the first is an almost purely idealistic dithyramb, the second is much more realistic and critical, even in those passages when he is speaking directly and not as if through the mouth of Coleridge. As a writer, Lamb was always at his happiest when his personalities could be set out in a partially dramatised form. Some self-consciousness clung to his style so long as he was writing directly in the first-person, but as soon as the naked "I" could be clothed—whether in the suit of Elia, of Coleridge, or of some other temporarily assumed character—the obstacle to easy self-revelation fell away. In regard to the Christ's Hospital memories, it is quite feasible that he had no sort of grievance or complaint to make; that he was altogether happy while at school; and that what few restrictions or disabilities irked others left the self-sufficing young Lamb unruffled. But it is more probable that the differing tone of the two pieces

D

of writing is not to be traced back to anything in the facts themselves, but belongs wholly to the change of form adopted by the author. Lamb was far from being at his best when writing straightforward narrative, just as it teased him to read it in other people's books; his early plain prose is clear and serviceable, but otherwise unremarkable. His Elia style relies very considerably upon dramatic effect, with all the light and shade which belong to good dramatic writing. At these times, Lamb's prose becomes immediately flexible and catches innumerable changing glints of character, until the style itself turns into a living thing.

When Talfourd was writing his Life of Lamb he asked one of the schoolfellows mentioned in *Christ's Hospital Five and Thirty Years Ago*—C. V. Le G—— (Charles Valentine Le Grice)—to jot down some recollections. In complying, Le Grice emphasised the mildness and amiability of Lamb as a boy, and his slow flat-footed manner of walking, which emphasised his generally staid appearance. He was frail, and this, together with the difficulty he experienced in uttering his words, set him a little apart from the rest of the young community, so that he hardly participated at all in the usual rough-and-tumble of a schoolboy's life. Considering these things, he might easily have become a butt for the young barbarians about him, though it would no doubt have been poor sport to bait one so equable as Charles Lamb. He alternated, Le Grice says, between the cloisters of his home in the Temple and the cloisters of the school at Newgate, obtruding upon none, offending none; himself the ideal type of Christ's Hospital boy, self-depicted as stealing along the streets "with all the self-concentration of a young monk". The wonder is that, bearing this character, it yet seems never to have occurred to any of his Blue-coat contemporaries to cold-shoulder him as a milksop. In the boy between the ages of seven and fifteen there must already have been some solid core of unusual quality which made him safe from any stigma of girlishness. All his life, however (and to his intense irritation), the epithet "gentle" clung to him. "I never heard his name mentioned", Le Grice wrote, "without the addition of Charles, although as there was no other boy of the name of Lamb, the addition was unnecessary; but there was an implied kindness in it, and it was a proof that his gentle manners excited that kindness." It must not be supposed that Lamb established no friendly relations with those who went to school with him. A good deal of evidence to the contrary is provided in his own work as well as in the fugitive writings of others. But always he must have turned upon the world and upon its occupants within range, that eye of shrewd appraisal which enabled him to detect—and in himself not least— something beyond reputed surface values.

§ 4

Before leaving Lamb's childhood years, further account must be taken of the boy's lingerings in and about the Temple, where the family continued to live until he was seventeen. That backwater of peace between Fleet Street and the Thames did at least as much to shape his disposition as any educational influence at Christ's. He rejoiced exceedingly in the Temple Gardens, at the foot of which the river then washed with no intervening embankment, but it was not nature that enthused him so much as man's handi-work in the gardens—the fountains and sundials, whose gradual disappearance he lamented. We can at any rate clearly visualise him as he used to stand amid the ample squares and green recesses of the lawyers' quarter, tiptoe before a sundial, watching the dark edge of shadow as it swallowed up the bright light of day without perceptible movement. And what child is not fascinated by fountains? Young Lamb had the additional delight of knowing their secret workings and, before a charmed audience of neighbouring infants, he would make the jetting waters rise and fall, wandering off from the Temple when that palled to the marble fountain in Lincoln's Inn where the water poured from the mouths of a quartette of cherubs.

Inside the family lodging there were other attractions, for if Mary Lamb had, as we know, the run of Samuel Salt's library, there is every reason to suppose that Charles had too. Curiously enough he gave no direct particulars of his early reading at home, but the beginnings of his love of the old authors must have been in Salt's "spacious closet of good old English reading" into which, he tells us, Mary was tumbled early, by accident or design. Salt himself was an imperturbable old man with a greater outside repu-tation for legal wisdom than the Lambs supposed he deserved. He could hardly be a hero to the elder John Lamb, who dressed him and took what care he could of his company manners, as well as handling such parts of the legal practice as Salt was either too busy or too uninformed to manage. The father's mild employer was but one among a number of old benchers whom the boy encountered with fluctuating sensations as they perambulated the terrace—stiff-wigged, gothic figures, some belching clouds of snuff, some shrouded in a melancholy quiet, some massive in bulk, some pale and spare, some cheery, some spiteful. Moving timidly but curiously on the outskirts of that odd company, Charles Lamb must have begun to acquire that liking for out-of-the-way humour and opinions, for people and affairs with a diverting twist, which was to give him his unique place among English authors.

CHAPTER TWO

CLERK AND BROTHER

§ 1

LAMB was fortunate in having a troop of
unangelic but incomparably useful guardian
presences in the foreground and the middle
distance while he was young: Mary and aunt Hetty
in the family circle; the Fields and Gladmans in
Hertfordshire; Salt and Yeats to ease him into the
Blue-coat ranks. The list does not end there. It is
supposed that he left school without definite plans
for the future, and there is no very clear evidence
as to what he was doing for the next twenty months.
But as from the autumn of 1791 there are no gaps
in our information, it can be confidently taken that
the references to Joseph Paice in *Modern Gallantry*
relate to the period following November 1789, when
Lamb finished at Christ's Hospital, a view supported
from other sources. Joseph Paice, a merchant with
premises in Bread Street Hill, took Lamb into his
office and taught him the rudiments of business,
a service amply repaid when his protégé, more than
thirty years later, immortalised him in print as the
flower of courtesy. There, for aught we know to the
contrary, Lamb remained until September 1791, when
he entered the Examiners' Office of the South Sea

Company, Paice being one of the directors. John
Lamb, the elder brother, was already permanently
installed there, but Charles left after twenty-three
weeks, during which he was paid at the rate of
10s. 6d. a week. For what responsible tasks he was
thus recompensed we have no means of knowing,
and it is unimportant beside the fact that the South
Sea House was to provide him in the end with much
more important than an embryonic salary—the beginnings of his age-long reputation as a writer. In
1820, when Lamb introduced himself in the cloak
of Elia to the readers of the *London Magazine*, he turned
back the page of memory to the five months spent with
the ill-fated South Sea Company. It seems likely that
he chose to review this relatively unimportant and
distant interlude because he had, a few days before,
picked up on a bookstall in Barbican a two-volume
collection of prose and verse by Henry Man, one of
the Company's officials remembered by Lamb. Though
that first essay contains several character-sketches in
Elia's best style it unfortunately does not enable us
to follow his own movements while in those apartments
of decayed magnificence where everything spoke of
glories of commerce that were crumbling almost before
they had been born. Concerning the clerks he describes,
Lamb had had two means of refreshing his memory,
through the calls he must from time to time have paid
to his brother John at the South Sea House, and
through the visits some of John's colleagues made to
the Lamb household. There was Evans, the cashier,
morose at his desk, but mellowing as the day drew
on. "The simultaneous sound of his well known rap
at the door with the stroke of the clock announcing
six, was a topic of never-failing mirth in the families

which this dear old bachelor gladdened with his presence. Then was his *forte*, his glorified hour. How would he chirp and expand, over a muffin!" Elia was as skilled in recreating inanimate things as in reviving persons, and apart from the extraordinary vividness of the great corridors and offices of the South Sea House as described in his pages, there is also the striking sense he gives of a departed age of giantesque clerks handling with ease the massive old account books which three men of the newer time could scarcely lift. Or was Lamb recalling these rubricated volumes as they had appeared to him at his first entry at the age of seventeen, a smaller edition of the frail creature below middle height that he was to be? His departure from the South Sea House coincided measurably with the death of Samuel Salt early in 1792. This was a critical event in the family history, and it does not appear that Mr. Lamb was in any other occupation for the remaining seven years of his life. Salt left him some £500, and £200 to Mrs. Lamb. Among the first changes necessitated by the old lawyer's death was the vacation of 2 Crown Office Row, and the Lambs moved, apparently, to 7 Little Queen Street, Holborn, one of the turnings obliterated when the Kingsway improvements were undertaken early in the present century.

On April 5, 1792, Charles Lamb found a footing in the East India House, where he remained for the next thirty-three years. There is nothing that lovers of Lamb could wish for more intensely than some detailed account of his business career. The records are so scanty in this connection and so full in relation to his non-professional experience that only by deliberately dwelling upon the point is it easy to realise how large a section of his life—more than half—was at the disposal of the East India Company. When Lamb does refer to office matters in his letters it is usually to complain in terms suggesting that he looked upon Leadenhall Street as the place of his ante-mortem sepulture. Yet it is hard to believe that, being Charles Lamb, he could have regarded accountancy as none other than an irksome means of earning his living, or have gone on from day to day for three and thirty years without finding in the work something other than a task job. Surely the keeping of accounts must have come alive under his hand. Still, we search his works in vain for some indication that he found joy in the worm of day-labour that orders most lives, though he does go so far as to hint that he devised an improved method of book-keeping. Since mankind as a whole is so addicted to the pretence that salaried work is altogether hateful, we may not go far wrons in suspecting that Lamb was inclined to harmles exaggeration on this topic. His progress in the service of the Company is proof of his efficiency. After the first three years of unpaid apprenticeship his salary increased at irregular intervals from £40 per annum in 1795 to £730 in 1825, when he retired at the early age of fifty on a substantial pension for faithful service. Nothing in these facts suggests a grudging attitude toward his employers nor anything in the nature of incompetence, notwithstanding his Elian declaration that accounts puzzled him and that he had no skill in figuring. Among the few pen-pictures of him as clerk that have come down to us from his colleagues are statements to the effect that he rarely did a full day's work at his desk, permitting himself to arrive late, to leave early, to spend a good deal of the day talking, to use office time (as we know from himself he used its stationery) for private correspondence. There are also tales concerning what appears like insolence to seniors. And yet against all this must be set what Lamb in one of his letters tells Manning about a certain clerk who arrived at the office drunk and, after thirty-six years' service, found his annual salary at once reduced from £600 to £100. We know further that, although the nominal office hours were absurdly few (9 till 3), Lamb sometimes worked there from 10 in the morning until 11 at night, and he noted to Wordsworth that he anticipated a good deal of such overtime.

By far the best description of Charles Lamb in harness at the East India House is that given by De Quincey, who, too impatient to wait to convey his letter of introduction to Lamb's home in the evening, presented it at the office. Having gained entrance to the building, he found himself in a room where, behind a high railing, sat six "quill-driving gentlemen" at lofty desks: "as if they supposed me a spy sent by some superior power to report upon the situation of affairs as surprised by me, they were all too profoundly immersed in their oriental studies to have any sense of my presence." When, breaking in upon their silent devotion, De Quincey announced himself and his business to the nearest clerk, he found it was Lamb, who smiled "a smile not to be forgotten". Then, the caller continues, occurred "an incident which to me . . . served to express the courtesy and delicate consideration of Lamb's manners. The seat upon which he sat was a very high one; so absurdly high, by the way, that I can imagine no possible use or sense in such an altitude. . . . To have sat still and stately

upon this aerial station, to have bowed condescend-
ingly from this altitude, would have been—not ludicrous indeed; performed by a very superb person,
and supported by a very superb bow, it might have
been vastly fine, and even terrifying to many young
gentlemen under sixteen; but it would have had an
air of ungentlemanly assumption. . . . Nobody who
knew Lamb can doubt how the problem was solved;
he began to dismount instantly; and, as it happened
that the very first *round* of his descent obliged him to
turn his back upon me as if for a sudden purpose of
flight, he had an excuse for laughing; which he did
heartily—saying, at the same time, something to this
effect: that I must not judge from first appearances;
that he should revolve upon me; that he was not going
to fly; and other facetiae, which challenged a general
laugh from the clerical brotherhood". To this account
(here pruned of much inflatory verbiage) may be
added part of an entry from Crabb Robinson's diary:
"The large room in the accountant's office at the East
India House is divided into boxes or compartments,
in each of which sat six clerks, Charles Lamb himself
in one. They are called Compounds. The meaning
of the word was asked one day, and Lamb said it was
'a collection of simples'." Outside these two references
little is to be gathered as to the physical conditions
in which Lamb worked, except that the office was
depressingly dark and candle-lit for half the year.

Such, then, was the background against which Lamb
for so long passed an existence he regarded as two-
thirds dead, "for Time that a man may call his own
is his Life, and hard work and thinking about it taints
even the leisure hours". How he at length escaped
and found another side to the picture must be told

later in its proper place and time. The only further point that need be remarked upon here in connection with his appointment, is that he was in all probability once more indebted to some of the old benchers of the Inner Temple, who established him in an at least secure position if not a congenial one. It was, furthermore, a post that enabled Charles and Mary after the first lean years to live comfortably and, from 1815, affluently. In their years of plenty they divided their substance with old acquaintances who became their pensioners, one of these being the Mrs. Reynolds who afforded Charles his first schooling. Even in regard to the early times there has been a tendency to overstress their poverty grossly—and there were always compensations for financial stringency. Like many another booklover, Lamb was content to tolerate clothes of the shabbiest sort so that he might acquire some coveted volume; and in after years both brother and sister were to look back with a pensive but sweet melancholy upon the occasion when Charles, after lengthy calculations between them, set out from Islington close upon ten o'clock one Saturday night in a sudden determination to knock up the bookseller in Covent Garden who had a folio Beaumont and Fletcher for sale. Those were days of doubt and trembling to live through, but heroic and lovely days to survey in retrospect.

We need to remember constantly that there were parts of Lamb's early life over which a romantic light appeared to flicker as he looked back upon them from the aridities of middle age. There was, for instance, the young affection for a Hertfordshire girl—probably a callow affair in actuality—which for the forty-six-year-old Elia had turned into a seven-year passionate love adventure. We do know that, out of selflessness as pure as could be, be abjured marriage, and, knowing this, we are readily disposed to share the touching regrets for his unborn children which make the *Dream Children* essay bring a lump into tender throats. Yet Charles Lamb was sufficiently a belated Elizabethan to express vicarious emotions with a semblance of deep conviction, and he could quite evidently be carried away by posthumously self-coloured visions of his own plain dead past. We do not detract from the merit of Lamb's altruism by holding that he was, for literary purposes and under the name of Elia, a conscious artificer who used only as much of actual fact as was adaptable to his purpose, and used that much only as far as it aided the pattern of his semi-imaginative creations. However potently our sympathies may be stirred at every remembrance that, for Mary's sake, he voluntarily resigned the experiences of husband-hood and fatherhood, the thought will keep breaking-in that if ever there was a divinely appointed bachelor Charles Lamb was he. So we may perhaps spare most of the pity we are instinctively moved to give as Elia sighs that he pined away seven of his goldenest years when he was "thrall to the fair hair, and fairer eyes, of Alice W——n". It was no doubt a pretty episode, but it is not likely to have been more than that—except in so far as every passing love affair is uniquely passionate for its principals, whether they are in Verona, Hertfordshire, or Hoxton. There are no facts to give concerning Charles' young romance, for we know nothing certainly about it. He wrote a few love poems in which the lady is called Anna, and references in letters at the time indicate that the relationship was at an end by the beginning of 1795, so that if Elia's recollections were to be taken seriously his passionate love must have begun when he was thirteen. The supposition by some commentators that Lamb became demented as a consequence of the break with Anna-Alice appears improbable, though the happening may have aggravated a predisposition to melancholy which for a while seriously assumed the upper hand during a period when he was cut off from his closest friend Coleridge. As to the identity of the girl, the evidence assembled by Mr. E. V. Lucas establishes that she was Ann Simmons, who lived near Blakesware and afterwards married a London pawn-broker named Bartrum. Writing to Coleridge at the end of 1796 Lamb closed the matter by saying that the folly (of love) had left him for ever, and asked that his verses when printed should no longer be called *Love Sonnets* but *Sketches*. For this decision, however, there was at that time a further and more distressing reason.

§ 2

After Samuel Salt died and Mr. Lamb was left with a small legacy but no occupation, Mary relied upon dressmaking as the chief means of amplifying whatever contribution her brother John was making to the household funds. Except for the little received from the South Sea House Charles did not begin to earn until he was twenty, when Salt had been dead three years.

John Lamb, the brother, was exceptionally well liked both by his mother and grandmother, and Charles loved and admired him though aware of his failings, but in the eyes of posterity he appears a somewhat unsympathetic character, notwithstanding Elia's en-

comium in *My Relations*. Something of a card, not
lacking in taste and culture, humane at least to
animals, John Lamb nevertheless seemed a boisterous
vulgarian to one at least of Charles' closest friends and
admirers. To us, it is John's selfishness that turns
uppermost, for there was no material reason why he
should not have assumed the main part of the family
responsibilities he was content to leave to others, and
perhaps even deliberately to evade when the need
was greatest. In the circumstances, and while Charles
was still an unpaid clerk, it is most probable that heavy
burdens fell upon the unrobust shoulders of Mary:
Mrs. Lamb was ailing; aunt Hetty, though good-
hearted and helpful, was a peculiar old body; and
the father was slipping into an exacting irritable second
childishness. But by the time they moved to Holborn,
Mary's mantua-making business was doing well enough
to justify her engaging a small girl apprentice.

At this stage, it is best to interpose an extract from
one of the London morning newspapers dated September 26, 1796:

On Friday afternoon the Coroner and a respectable
Jury sat on the body of a Lady in the neighbourhood
of Holborn, who died in consequence of a wound from
her daughter the preceding day. It appeared by the
evidence adduced, that while the family were preparing
for dinner, the young lady seized a case knife laying on
the table, and in a menacing manner pursued a little girl,
her apprentice, round the room; on the eager calls of her
helpless infirm mother to forbear, she renounced her
first object, and with loud shrieks approached her parent.

The child by her cries quickly brought up the landlord
of the house, but too late—the dreadful scene presented
to him the mother lifeless, pierced to the heart, on the

chair, her daughter yet wildly standing over her with the fatal knife, and the venerable old man, her father, weeping by her side, himself bleeding at the forehead from the effects of a severe blow he received from one of the forks she had been madly hurling about the room.

For a few days prior to this the family had observed some symptoms of insanity in her, which had so much increased on the Wednesday evening, that her brother early the next morning went in quest of Dr. Pitcairn— had that gentleman been met with, the fatal catastrophe had, in all probability been prevented.

It seems the young Lady had been once before, in her earlier years, deranged, from the harassing fatigues of too much business.—As her carriage towards her mother was ever affectionate in the extreme, it is believed that to the increased attentiveness, which her parents' infirmities called for by day and night, is to be attributed the present insanity of this ill-fated young woman.

It has been stated in some of the Morning Papers, that she has an insane brother also in confinement—this is without foundation.

The Jury of course brought in their Verdict, Lunacy.

Little need be added to the *Morning Chronicle* reporter's description of the tragedy at 7 Little Queen Street, and it is idle to speculate upon the difference that would have been made both to the Lambs' family history and to English literature if Dr. Pitcairn had been at home when Charles went on the Thursday morning to summon him. The newspaper's repudiation of the rumour of an insane brother was only partially true. Charles had been confined in an asylum for six weeks at the end of 1795, a piece of information given to Coleridge in the earliest of Lamb's letters to be preserved. Mary had been "ill" (and tended by Charles) some twelve months before his own mental breakdown. There is also some ground for thinking that grandmother Field intervened between Lamb and Ann on account of a family taint of insanity. But when the catastrophe came it was not the mature handsome robust John who took charge of affairs. He was of opinion that Mary should be sent to Bedlam for the rest of her life, but Charles had other views and it was he who prevailed. Calculating that they could manage to spare fifty or sixty pounds (about one-third of the household incomings) for Mary to be cared for, he arranged that she should be taken in charge at a private residence at Islington, pending the time when she should be well enough to go into lodgings—which she did in the following spring, at Hackney. Though Mary speedily recovered from her worst frenzy, she suffered relapses at intervals for the remainder of her long life, and was compelled to spend increasingly lengthy periods under restraint. In her rational periods however—and these sometimes lasted for several years —she was a woman of uncommon sensibility, as her literary works show. Within a few days after the tragic end of Mrs. Lamb, Mary appears to have had a clear recollection of what transpired. Charles told Coleridge that the remembrance was "awful to her mind, and impressive (as it must be to the end of life) but temper'd with religious resignation, and the reasonings of a sound judgment, which in this early stage knows how to distinguish between a deed committed in a transient fit of frenzy, and the terrible guilt of a Mother's murder". Aunt Hetty, whom Lamb found on the first evening lying insensible, quickly recovered and went to live with a rich gentlewoman cousin who, after a few months, found the old lady unbearably "indolent and mulish" and was glad to return her to

E

the Lambs, with whom at the end of 1796 she moved from Little Queen Street to 45 Chapel Street, Pentonville, for the short remainder of her life. One of the chief consolations during this time of horror was found in the number of friends who rallied to the help of the family in various practical ways. Consolation of another but not less valued sort was vouchsafed by Coleridge from Bristol. He was for several years Charles Lamb's most frequent correspondent, and his religious letter (immediately after the disaster) counselling patience and resignation was warmly acknowledged by Lamb as "an inestimable treasure". Soon after, Coleridge's letters were being read by brother and sister together, and Charles was entering upon metaphysical arguments with their writer in regard to what he stigmatised as a tendency on the poet's side to indulge in pagan conceits under the guise of Christian piety. This quick resumption of a critical interest in larger questions confirms Lamb's own remark that his mind preserved a state of tranquillity throughout the period of distress. It is not surprising to know that he came closer to being a religious man, in the formal accepted sense, during this time than at any other; yet the ability to accept a ready-made religion was not in him. His temper was altogether too curiously sceptical ever to embrace a set of crystallised dogmas, but if, without dogma, a man may be inherently religious, Charles Lamb was so. He had a sense of the divinity behind phenomena and the idea of duty was insistent in his personal conduct throughout life. Whether Lamb was categorically "a Christian" is not a problem for us to attempt to solve; we must be content to say that he behaved consistently as a great many Christians would be the better for behaving.

When immediate anxieties as to Mary's condition were temporarily allayed, old Mr. Lamb became the most pressing weight to be borne by his younger son. He had begun to break up as soon as he was involuntarily released from duties in the Temple, and this decline was inevitably accelerated by the wound he received on the day of his wife's death. Yet his own sufferings were mitigated by the failing of memory, and he was playing cribbage with one of Charles' friends while the coroner's inquest was being conducted across the road, a merciful oblivion having settled upon his mind. Again it was Charles who bore the brunt of his father's fractiousness when the old man, probably unawares and certainly without malice, uttered his cruelties. It became Lamb's practice to hasten home from East India House to spend the evening playing cards with his father, who grew accustomed to this anodyne and demanded it with as fretful persistency as a drug-taker might use when craving for opiates. Charles was compelled to hurry through his evening meal so that Mr. Lamb might set to cribbage with him until bedtime. Here is a brief account of a typical night, taken from a letter to Coleridge in December 1796: "I am starving at the India House, near 7 o'clock without my dinner, and so it has been and will be almost all the week. I get home at night o'er wearied, quite faint,—and then to CARDS with my father, who will not let me enjoy a meal in peace—but I must conform to my situation, and I hope I am, for the most part, not unthankful. I am got home at last, and, after repeated games at Cribbage have got my father's leave to write awhile: with difficulty got it, for when I expostulated about playing any more, he very aptly replied, 'if you won't play with me, you might as well not come home at all'. The answer was unanswerable, and I set to afresh." If this, with its remarkable combination of irony and stoical submission, cannot be taken as an unpremeditated self-portrait of a truly religious man there is little purpose in striving after religion, or even after philosophy. Lamb had determined that Mary should not be brought back into the household so long as the father continued alive: he feared the possible consequence of a reunion of the two, and of the memories that might be started into an appalling new activity by the meeting. Accordingly, it was not until after John Lamb the elder died in April 1799 that Mary returned to live in the same house as Charles, she having in the meantime experienced two recurrences of her malady. Their father's last days had been increasingly pitiful, and are described in what is written concerning Lovel in Elia's essay on the benchers of the Inner Temple.

As it is neither possible not necessary to detail in this study the whole course of Mary's illnesses, the subject can be dismissed for the present with the affecting account given in an early memoir by Lamb's friend B. W. Procter (Barry Cornwall). He says that whenever, by irritability or a change of manner, the oncoming of one of her fits of insanity was announced "Lamb would take her, under his arm, to Hoxton Asylum. It was very affecting to encounter the young brother and his sister walking together (weeping together) on this painful errand; Mary herself, although sad, very conscious of the necessity for temporary separation from her only friend. They used to carry a strait jacket with them". The authenticity of this account is confirmed by another member of the Lamb circle, though Procter a little overdid the pathetic note by writing of Charles as Mary's only friend. He was the closest, most devoted and most cherished, but neither of the two ever had sound cause to complain of a paucity of good friends. Mary on one occasion seems to have thought their friends were few, though Charles' complaints were altogether otherwise, and with every reason.

CHAPTER THREE

THE FRIEND

§ 1

WITH threescore friends and ten and an office to go to six days a week, a man can have little time to give to literature. From his middle twenties until death had thinned the ranks many years later, Lamb was constantly beset by a cloud of friendly witnesses whom he only half-humorously reproached in print and in letters for their tireless pursuit of his company. He could neither eat nor write without an attendance of droppers-in, and he was so far from being curmudgeonly that he disliked their going more than their coming. But while he had the characteristics of a born crony he also loved solitude and the unvocal company of books, and the pressure of visitors at length drove him to hire a room away from home where he could be tolerably sure of enjoying aloneness when he desired it. This was in 1806, and, although Lamb did not long insulate himself in that apartment (for which he paid 3s. a week), there came a later occasion when he was to have in a surprising way similar opportunities for quiet in more spacious circumstances. In 1814 (Charles and Mary were then living in another part of the Temple—Mitre Court Buildings) they one day heard a cat crying. Describing the incident in a letter to a young friend, Mary said that it "seemed to proceed from the garrets adjoining to ours, and only separated from ours by a locked door on the further side of my brother's bedroom, which you know was the little room at the top of the kitchen stairs. We had the lock forced and let poor puss out from behind a panel of the wainscot, and she lived with us from that time, for we were in gratitude bound to keep her, as she had introduced us to four untenanted, unowned rooms, and by degrees we have taken possession of these unclaimed apartments—first putting up lines to dry our clothes, then moving my brother's bed into one of these, more commodious than his own room. And last winter, my brother being unable to pursue a work he had begun, owing to the kind interruptions of friends who were more at leisure than himself, I persuaded him that he might write at his ease in one of these rooms, as he could not then hear the door knock, or hear himself denied to be at home, which was sure to make him call out and convict the poor maid in a fib. Here, I said, he might be almost really not at home. So I put in an old grate, and made him a fire in the largest of these garrets, and carried in one table and one chair, and bid him write away, and consider himself as much alone as if he were in a new lodging in the midst of Salisbury Plain, or any other wide, unfrequented place where he could expect few visitors to break in upon his solitude. I left him quite delighted with his new acquisition, but in a few hours he came down again with a sadly dismal face. He could do nothing, he said, with those bare whitewashed walls before his eyes. He could not write in that dull unfurnished prison. The next day, before he came home from his office, I had gathered up various bits of old carpeting to cover the floor; and, to a little break the blank look of the bare walls, I hung up a few old prints that used to ornament the kitchen; and after dinner, with great boast of what improvement I had made, I took Charles once more into his new study. A week of busy labours followed, in which I think you would not have disliked to have been our assistant. My brother and I almost covered the walls with prints, for which purpose he cut out every print from every book in his old library, coming in every now and then to ask my leave to strip a fresh poor author—which he might not do you know, without my permission, as I am elder sister. There was such pasting, such consultation where their portraits, and where the series of pictures from Ovid, Milton, and Shakespeare would show to most advantage, and in what obscure corner authors of humbler note might be allowed to tell their stories. . . . To conclude this long story about nothing, the poor despised garret is now called the print room, and is become our most favorite sitting room."

In the days before Lamb's friends could hive in his rooms, he and Coleridge foregathered at a haunt in Newgate Street, variously referred to in correspondence as the *Salutation* Tavern, the *Salutation* Coffee House, and the *Salutation and Cat*. Any lively-minded man who recalls the sensations of young manhood will well understand, from the references in Lamb's letters, what those prolonged nights meant to the two eager youths (they were little more: Lamb nineteen, Coleridge twenty-two) just discovering life. Then, as always, Coleridge was a marvellous talker and, as such, was an asset to the landlord of the tavern. To Lamb—despite their having been to school together—Coleridge served as an eye-opener during their meetings at the *Salutation*. They talked poetry there, perhaps actually composed it, while consuming welch-rabbits and egghot; to add that metaphysical discussion occupied a large part of the hours they passed together is unnecessary—Coleridge and metaphysics were united in the womb. When Coleridge, entangled equally by philosophy and young women, left London, there began the life-long correspondence between him and Lamb, occasionally interrupted by misunderstandings —sometimes due to Coleridge's touchiness and sometimes to the eruptive influence of other acquaintances. Most that is good in the practical part of philosophy appears to have been absorbed by Lamb, while to Coleridge were left the husks of the theoretical profundities; it is a pity that these did not save him from indulgence in an unadult and most unphilosophic propensity for petulance and the adoption of a patronising air to some who were far from being his mental inferiors. He wrote a poem (*This Lime-tree Bower my Prison*) containing lines of unsolicited condolence with Lamb, whom he addressed with maddening and semi-imbecile iteration as "my gentle-hearted Charles". The poem is important, not for any poetic merit, but because it stung Lamb to good-humored but emphatic protest (at the age of twenty-five) in two letters. His objection was not merely to Coleridge's making him ridiculous in print, but also to his doing it in such poor verse. Suggesting, more than playfully, that "gentle-hearted" could be too easily interpreted to mean "poor-spirited", he urged that in another edition the epithet should be changed to "drunken, dog, ragged-head, seld-shaven, odd-eyed, stuttering" or any other that would have appeared to the victim to be more properly in character. That Coleridge's feeling for Lamb and his sister was deep and genuine cannot be doubted, but affection to be lastingly bearable needs to be tempered by discretion and good taste, qualities available to this particular poet only in those hours when he was indubitably and miraculously great. Still, Lamb believed him to be a very good man, and to Coleridge must go the credit for being the first to stir his friend actively to authorship. John Lamb (the younger) brutally insisted that Coleridge was the cause of Charles' attack of insanity, by communicating his "damned foolish sensibility and melancholy", but Charles came nearer than anyone else to capturing a volatile and evasive personality in a phrase when he described Coleridge to Wordsworth as "an Archangel a little damaged".

From a statement in the open *Letter of Elia to Robert Southey* it is evident that Southey was sometimes present at the convivial and speculative evenings at the *Salutation and Cat*; and we learn also from that document that among the subjects then discussed was Pantisocracy, the hare-brained scheme for setting-up an ideal community on the banks of the Susquehannah to which Coleridge and Southey and a number of disciples were within an ace of committing themselves in practice. Though Southey was, at the time, perhaps the most eminent of the group, he played only a small part in the life of Charles Lamb, and notwithstanding that a number of friendly letters passed between them there was at moments a latent touch of asperity in their relationship, and this came to a head when Lamb a little pettily took exception to some of Southey's printed comments on *The Essays of Elia*, and replied in the communication mentioned above. The *Letter*, as a piece of composition, is not unworthy of Elia, and its biographical interest is increased by the partially annotated catalogue of his friends inserted by the writer to confound Southey. The most illustrious of these was Wordsworth, who received some of the finest of Lamb's letters, though the two were not very closely intimate—probably because they were for most part of their lives separated, first by the breadth and then by the length of England. They were also temperamentally diverse. Wordsworth would have welcomed a little less of what he regarded as frivolity in Lamb, and Lamb a little less solemnity in Wordsworth. Of the two, so far as their appreciation of one another's writings was concerned, Lamb was the more critical —and the more daring. When Wordsworth sent him the second edition of the *Lyrical Ballads* at the beginning of 1801, Lamb acknowledged the book in the excellent letter containing in its second half the famous eulogy of London provoked by an invitation to stay with the Wordsworths at Dove Cottage, Grasmere. The letter opens with a lengthy commentary upon the *Lyrical Ballads*, giving full marks to Coleridge's *Ancient Mariner* and Wordsworth's *Mad Mother* and *Tintern Abbey*. If he had put discretion before critical candour and stopped there, all might have been well, even if Wordsworth had chanced to react a little frigidly to the preference shown for the *Ancient Mariner*, but Lamb added a few strictures—upon the preface to the volumes (one of Wordsworth's pet pieces) and upon a few of the poems—in which he suggested the presence of vulgar satire, coarse epithets (aesthetically, not morally, coarse) and prosiness. In regard to this last, Lamb offered a few admirable observations on the writer's craft, and if Wordsworth had not been so outraged he might have benefited all but his best poetry by heeding Lamb's remarks. The sequel is set down in a letter to Manning in the following month, where Charles quotes a selection of Wordsworth's counter-comments sent in a posthaste reply. This letter cannot but add to one's admiration and respect for Lamb both as a man and a critic. He was neither timidified by the heavy guns of humourless self-assertion trained upon him from the Lake District (for Coleridge also had started up in drop-jawed amazement that Lamb should see spots on the face of a god) nor led by irritation to pretend to Manning that the best things in the *Lyrical Ballads* were other than very good indeed. There can have been few instances in the history of criticism where a contemporary so closely anticipated the considered judgments of posterity, and the laugh is all on the side of Lamb, whose mild indignation in the matter was aroused—now and on a later occasion—by Wordsworth's assumption that he could have written like Shakespeare if he had thought it worth while to do so. Said Lamb to Manning: "after one had been reading Shakespeare twenty of the best years of one's life, to have a fellow start up, and prate about some unknown quality, which Shakespeare possessed in a degree inferior to Milton and somebody else!!" For some of Wordsworth's later poetry Lamb had almost unmeasured praise, and he came to have a high opinion of his personal nobility. On the publication of *The Excursion* in 1814 Wordsworth desired that the poem should be reviewed by Lamb and, the matter having been arranged with the editor of the *Quarterly*, the review was duly written with much painstaking labour, this being a department of journalism in which Lamb had no natural aptitude.

As, in the meantime, he had written with spontaneous enthusiasm to Wordsworth that he had had a day in heaven while reading *The Excursion*—"the noblest conversational poem I ever read"—we may judge of his dismay on discovering, when the long-delayed review appeared, that the editor had drastically altered the article, not only by reducing it considerably in length, but also (according to its author's complaint) by substituting for every warm expression "a nasty cold one". Marked by a certain staidness (Lamb's attitude toward Wordsworth when in his company is said to have been "almost respectful") the friendship between the two men and their families was not injured by the sparks now and again struck out by the clashing of the two geniuses. Wordsworth was a great man: Lamb knew it; Wordsworth also knew it, and his illimitable but really lovable egoism was shrewdly noted by Crabb Robinson when attending a party at the Lambs' at which the two poets were present: "I heard at one time Coleridge quoting Wordsworth's verses, and W. quoting *not* Coleridge's but his own."

Wordsworth outlived Lamb by a good many years and he was asked to write the epitaph to be cut on Lamb's tombstone. He did so readily, and sent it with an explanatory letter saying that although the poem was long he thought it might not be unusable on that account if it were engraved in double column. A briefer epitaph was chosen for the stone.

§ 2

There were several assured "immortals" among Lamb's friends. Upon at least one other he conferred immortality by being his friend. But for George Dyer's life-size appearance in Lamb's letters and essays there is no reason to suppose that posterity (other than the antiquarian section of it) would have heard of him. To begin plainly with a person who is invariably picturesque as we see him—George Dyer was born at Wapping in 1755, and was thus Lamb's senior by twenty years. He was educated at Christ's Hospital and Emmanuel College, Cambridge. After some years as a school usher and private tutor he turned to literature of the unpretentious grub-street kind, undertaking almost any task that publishers were prepared to give him, and becoming a martyr-of-letters by injuring his eyesight in too close application to these labours. He wrote history and biography as well as poetry. This bare account gives us no reason to suppose that Dyer would play an important part among the intellectuals of his day, yet he was a very star among them, shining unaware for others and not for himself. It was all because of his innocence, which was so innocent as to be superlatively beautiful. Some people have said that he was humourless; he was—if an unblemished new-born babe on the plains of heaven is also to be called humourless. In truth it is at once meaningless and slanderous to use the word at all of George Dyer. It suggests a fault in him, whereas he was flawless. But every one of our customary meaning-ful epithets fails and becomes null and void when applied to him. Not that he was either heroic or angelic. He was George Dyer.

His first direct appearance in the present story was on December 5, 1808, when Lamb wrote to give him the local news and gossip, and particularly to complain of the number of painters who were straying from their own art and competing against the already over-numerous tribe of struggling poets. There must have been earlier letters which have not been preserved, for Dyer had been off-stage in Lamb's correspondence since 1796, and anecdotes concerning him are a recurrent feature in the letters. The long-impending publication of George's own poems is one of the principal topics, culminating in the catastrophe described by Lamb in the letter to Manning dated December 27, 1800: "At length George Dyer's phrenesis has come to a crisis; he is raging and furiously mad. I waited upon the heathen, Thursday was a se'nnight; the first symptom which struck my eye and gave me incontrovertible proof of the fatal truth was a pair of nankeen pantaloons four times too big for him, which the said heathen did pertinaciously affirm to be new. They were absolutely ingrained with the accumulated dirt of ages; but he affirmed them to be clean. He was going to visit a lady that was nice about those things, and that's the reason he wore nankeen that day. And then he danced, and capered, and fidgeted, and pulled up his pantaloons, and hugged his intolerable flannel vestment closer about his poetic loins; anon he gave it loose to the zephyrs which plentifully insinuate their tiny bodies through every crevice, door, window or wainscot, expressly formed for the exclusion of such impertinents. Then he caught at a proof sheet, and catched up a laundress's bill instead—made a dart at Blomfield's Poems, and threw them in agony aside. I could not bring him to one direct reply; he could not maintain his jumping mind in a right line for the tithe of a moment by Clifford's Inn clock. He must go to the printers immediately—the most unlucky accident—

he had struck off five hundred impressions of his Poems, which were ready for delivery to subscribers, and the Preface must all be expunged. There were eighty pages of Preface, and not till that morning had he discovered that in the very first page of said Preface he had set out with a principle of Criticism fundamentally wrong, which vitiated all his following reasoning. The Preface must be expunged, although it cost him £30—the lowest calculation, taking in paper and printing! In vain have his real friends remonstrated against this Midsummer madness. George is as obstinate as a Primitive Christian—and wards and parries off all our thrusts with one unanswerable fence;—'Sir, it's of great consequence that the world is not misled!' "

The precise nature of the supposed critical enormity was unapparent to anyone but Dyer, though he carried out his determination to cancel the original preface and substitute another. Lamb remarked elsewhere upon George's "utter ignorance that the world don't care a pin about his odes and criticisms, a fact which everybody knows but himself". Almost everyone who knew him had good stories to tell concerning George Dyer and his harmless follies. They all poked fun at him, but never in malice; if he was a target for their jokes he yet was not the victim of ill-natured ridicule, and they all rejoiced to have him married at seventy by an admirable widow who tended him with affectionate care until he died, quite blind, in his eighty-sixth year. George Dyer's irruptions into the pages of Elia (*Oxford in the Vacation* and *Amicus Redivivus*) show Charles Lamb fitted with material exactly suited to his temper and style. The second of the two essays named puts on record what must surely have been the most surprising adventure in even George Dyer's unpredictable career—his tumbling into the New River outside Lamb's cottage at Islington. But Dyer dressed for the world's eye in *The Essays of Elia* is a trifle formalised as compared with the George who appears in undress in the letters of Lamb. When that has been said, however, we recall the concluding words of *Oxford in the Vacation:* "On the Muses' hill he is happy, and good, as one of the Shepherds on the Delectable Mountains; and when he goes about with you to show you the halls and colleges, you think you have with you the Interpreter at the House Beautiful." No man could hope to deserve a lovelier epitaph; and if those words had been chiselled above George Dyer's grave, this would be one of the rare instances when a man would have no cause to blush beneath his own tombstone.

§ 3

Lamb's friends might be separated into two groups, according to whether they were notabilities in their own right, or ordinary people distinguished by proximity to him. Their total number is too considerable for more than a few cursory glances here.

In addition to the three Lake Poets already spoken of in some detail—Wordsworth, Coleridge, Southey —there were the writers whom hostile reviewers of the day hastily lumped together as the Cockney School. The composition of the Cockney School need not, indeed cannot, be nicely determined, since in those days, from a particular politico-literary standpoint, any opponent (or supposed opponent) could be labelled Cockney with the same abusive intent as is nowadays displayed by the use of the label Bolshevik. There were, however, in this vaguely defined group, or

F

on its confines, Leigh Hunt, William Hazlitt, William Godwin, Thomas Hood and others of minor note— all familiars of Lamb—and Keats, who was now and again in the same company as Lamb, without either being much drawn to the other. Of those just enumerated, Hazlitt was the most familiar friend, and if he had earned no fame on his own account we might claim it for him on the ground that he was once knocked down by Charles Lamb's brother John while they were arguing about pictures. Hazlitt was always a mettlesome creature, forever trailing his coat in the most provocative manner possible, and upholding active antagonism as one of the first duties of man. In social and intellectual relationships he was adamant, whereas Lamb was infinitely pliable. There was never any counterchange or approximation of characteristics as a product of the intercourse between the two essayists. Hazlitt, so some of his acquaintances said, was not averse to borrowing good things from the lips of Lamb, yet it cannot be alleged that the genius of Hazlitt owed anything to that of his friend; they were both originals. Hazlitt was of the conventionally unconventional brood that swarms wherever literary persons assemble in any age: his originality was confined to his writing; in personal bearing he struck the altogether unoriginal attitude of expecting the world to mould itself to him. Lamb was satisfied to accept (or to appear to accept) the shape and colour of his environment, though in so doing he was often, subtly, a moulding and modifying agent. It was easier to fall out with Hazlitt than to retain his friendship; in this respect Charles Lamb made occasional slips, but the two were never seriously alienated. The tie between them was strengthened by Mary Lamb's friendship with Sarah

Stoddart who, in 1808, became the first Mrs. William Hazlitt. There had been a long-standing acquaintance-ship between the Stoddarts and the Lambs before the first of the surviving letters to Sarah, in which Mary gave prudent advice about the way to treat lovers, and also in a quaint phrase mentions a serious conver-sation she had had with Sarah's sister-in-law "while she was eating a bit of cold mutton in our kitchen".

More or less everyone in literary London at that time passed within the orbit of Leigh Hunt, in his capacity as a leading political journalist and an editor. Some of Lamb's earliest essays came out in Leigh Hunt's paper, *The Reflector*, and the two were of one mind in regard to such well-hated contemporary figures as the Prince Regent, for lampooning whom Leigh Hunt went to prison for two years. It was chiefly on account of Hunt's radical views that opprobrium fell upon the other writers who, by the elastic exercise of political spleen, could be lashed together as low-down Cockneys. Just as Hazlitt's writings are disproportionately over-shadowed by Lamb's, so Leigh Hunt's suffer by com-parison with both. He is still remembered, however, for his *Autobiography*—one of the best in English literature.

Time has tarnished the reputation of William Godwin more than that of any of his contemporaries. As the author of *Political Justice* and the apostle of free thought, Godwin was idolised by the advanced and anathe-matised by the conservative. Seen across a century he appears to us to have merited neither mark of distinc-tion, nor the title of "the Philosopher" seriously given by his friends. He flits across the screen of Lamb's life and would no doubt have taken a more important place upon it if (after Mary Wollstone-

craft's death) he had not had the misfortune to marry
a widow (Mrs. Clairmont) who did not encourage his
former cronies. She was of the type we now describe
as "possessive women", and Lamb came as near to
hating her as was possible to one of his temperament.
The account he gave Rickman of Godwin's courting
is Lamb with a dash of vinegar: "The Lady is a Widow
with green spectacles and one child, and the Professor
is grown quite juvenile. He bows when he is spoken to,
and smiles without occasion, and wriggles as fantastically as Malvolio, and has more affectation than a
canary bird pluming his feathers, when he thinks
somebody looks at him. He lays down his spectacles,
as if in scorn, and takes 'em up again from necessity,
and winks that she mayn't see he gets sleepy about
eleven o'clock. You never saw such a philosophic
coxcomb, nor any one play the Romeo so unnaturally."
So much for the erstwhile champion of free-love, a
second time married at forty-five and to the mother
of Jane Clairmont.

Today everyone knows and no one cares about such
former eminences as Godwin, though a century ago
only a courageous and uncommonly perceptive prophet
would have dreamt of forecasting so strange a reversal
of values as has now made Henry Crabb Robinson,
in our eyes, worth a wilderness of Godwins. Robinson
was born at Bury St. Edmunds in 1775, and was thus
the same age as Lamb. He travelled much abroad in
his twenties and came back to England hoping to
find some literary occupation. John Walter the second,
editor and proprietor of *The Times*, sent Crabb Robinson to Altona at the beginning of 1807 to collect and
winnow such information as he could gather about the
Napoleonic campaign, and in this capacity he ranked

as a foreign correspondent of the paper. In the following year he became "a sort of foreign editor" of *The Times* and occupied a room in the editorial offices in Printing House Square. In this and other ways he served the paper until 1809, being treated by Walter rather as a friend than as a salaried journalist. Robinson then turned his attention to the law, was called to the Bar in 1813, and eventually became leader on the Norfolk circuit. The purpose of detailing these facts here is to offset a too general modern impression that Crabb was a literary gossip and nothing more. He has achieved posthumous fame because he kept a diary, but outside this he was, like Pepys, an accomplished and useful person. His genuine interest in literature and literary society was not matched by any creative or originative power as a writer, and he was sensible enough not to try to force his capabilities beyond their natural range. He accordingly set himself to act as a recorder to the congregation of geniuses of varying stature among whom he had the pleasure and good fortune to move on cordial terms. By character and temperament Crabb Robinson was the antithesis of Pepys; he was liker to (though somewhat livelier than) John Evelyn. As a diarist he had the right flair for noting down those revelatory trifles that at once illuminate the recesses of personality. For many years he was a privileged household friend of the Lambs and his diaries and journals add indispensably to the available information concerning Charles and Mary; he was, almost, their Boswell (and they were but two of the many literary characters he knew and wrote about in an equally enlightening fashion). He long survived them both, and after Charles' death offered to make what was a generous financial provision for

Mary, by whom he was affectionately called "Crabby". The diary and journals are continuously interesting and charming—more for their convincing effect of a day-by-day reproduction of life's littlenesses than for any opportunity they offer for picking out plums of humour and striking incident. Often Robinson put down the veriest trifles, yet they all count toward a finished picture. Part of one entry may be quoted, though it is not to be read as a typical example of the diarist's manner: "A day of great pleasure, Charles Lamb and I walked to Enfield by Southgate, after an early breakfast in his chambers. . . . After tea, Lamb and I returned. The whole day most delightfully fine, and the scenery very agreeable. Lamb cared for the walk more than the scenery, for the enjoyment of which he seems to have no great susceptibility. His great delight, even in preference to a country walk, is a stroll in London. The shops and the busy streets, such as Thames Street, Bankside, etc., are his great favourites. He, for the same reason, has no relish for landscape paintings. But his relish for historic painting is exquisite. Lamb's peculiarities are very interesting. He had not much conversation. He hummed tunes, I repeated Wordsworth's *Daffodils*, of which I am become very fond." Lamb wrote few letters to Crabb Robinson, and most of those were short; the shortest of them all is also one of the most famous he ever penned—on the day of his retirement: "I have left the d——d India House for ever! Give me great joy. C. Lamb". Robinson also displays that other desirable quality in a diarist, candour. In his frequent reports of evening parties he does not fail to express his plain opinion of those present. To say that he was a good hater would give a wrong impression of the man; he had a strong sense of propriety and would have thought it improper to hate; but he was a hearty disliker and if, imitating Lamb, he had written a series of *Popular Fallacies* Robinson would assuredly have coined (in order to refute) the fallacy "Love me, love my friend". Not that he was officiously censorious; but he was as incapable of insincerity as Lamb, without Lamb's urbanity and nicely balanced diplomacy. It was on this account that Mary once mildly scolded Crabb Robinson by saying, "You are rich in friends. We cannot afford to cast off ours because they are not all we wish." Such a sentence as the last is curious as coming from one who was, we should think, encompassed by a superfluity of friends. At any rate, as we have seen, that was Charles' view; they stuck to him, he tells us, like burrs: "his *intimados*, to confess a truth, were in the world's eye a ragged regiment."

The regiment was ragged in a special sense, however. In its ranks were as many of the eminently respectable as of the more bohemian kind, for Lamb was a true gentleman—equally at home with lords and sweeps, neither deferring to the one nor condescending to the other. Few of us escape being snobs, if only in the effort we make to demonstrate to ourselves that we are free from snobbery; it was otherwise with Lamb. He was an innate leveller, yet took no pains to be so. This is remarkable considering that at first he had little taste for company of any kind, but we must remember that while running about as a boy in the Temple he cut across the tracks of all sorts and conditions of men in circumstances where there were no obtrusive social divisions. Living in the same domicile as Samuel Salt and having the run of his library must have given him a certain confident ease in the company of "superiors",

while, at Christ's Hospital, he rubbed elbows with a
curiously assorted mannikin community. Add to this
that, in after years, through one of his old schoolfellows, James White, he was literally the associate of
sweeps. Elia told the story of White's yearly supper
at Smithfield for the London chimney-sweeps, at which
Lamb used to officiate as one of the stewards. Through
White, also, he met an indiscriminate company of
personal acquaintances during the youthful years of
their intimacy, and the *Letters of Falstaff*, by which
James White is still occasionally remembered, were
fabricated with certain undefined assistance from
Charles Lamb.

Some of the friends who were prominent in the early
part of Lamb's life diminish in importance afterwards,
though few of them disappear. White was one of these,
so also was Charles Lloyd. Coleridge, round about
1796, developed an extravagantly enthusiastic admiration for Lloyd (a member of the well-known banking
family) to whom he was then acting as tutor. It is
enough to say that the pupil quickly failed, in Coleridge's opinion, to live up to the idealistic role for which
he had (quite unsuitably) been cast, and that before
long he was being reproached for causing a breach
between Coleridge and Lamb. Probably Coleridge's
fatuity was to blame more than any intentional
duplicity in Lloyd, though Lamb apparently at one
time thought otherwise. The friendship between
Charles Lloyd and Lamb may have been more important in the latter's life than we now have means of
knowing, since most of Lamb's letters to this correspondent were destroyed. By lovers of Charles Lamb's
work Lloyd is likely to be best remembered because
he stirred that interest in Quakers which gave grace

to one of the choicest parts of Elia. Lamb tells Coleridge, "Lloyd has kindly left me for a keep-sake, John Woolman": this was the *Journal* of the American "Friend", a classic of Quaker literature and one of the books Lamb loved best. To Robert Lloyd, Charles' younger brother, Lamb was a good friend and wrote several adviceful and characteristically sensible letters. It was through Charles Lloyd that Thomas Manning, with whom Lamb frequently corresponded, came into the circle—to be from that time forward one of Lamb's most admired and most loved friends. To "Mister Manning, Teacher of Mathematics and the Black Arts" at Cambridge (later he went to China for a period) was addressed from time to time a budget of news and gossip relating to Lamb's doings and associates, and from this sequence of letters can be gathered a good many of the amusing and intimate details that have made the life of Charles Lamb one of the most fascinating in literary history. So far as Manning himself is concerned there is nothing to add. In Lamb's opinion he was an incomparable genius, too lazy to realise his powers; whether this was indeed so, or whether it was the too-admiring illusion of a friend, there is no means of discovering. The illusion, if it was that, lasted for thirty-six years and was only dissipated by death—a history very different from the traditional fate of illusions. It should be observed further, that to at least one other member of the circle Manning appeared to be a wonderful man with "extraordinary and very peculiar powers".

If there were any present intention of painting a satisfactory group-portrait of the entire company of Lamb's *intimados*, it would be imperative to refer at length to the Burneys, the Moxons, the Bartons, the

Allsops, and more than a score others. In so far as any of these is of special importance to the main narrative of his life they will take their place elsewhere in these pages. There is a constant danger, in writing about Lamb, of creating the impression that he was "the little friend of all the world", neither giving nor receiving offence from any quarter. This, certainly, would be a false impression. If he had enemies they were probably among those who knew him least and had partisan reasons for antagonism; nevertheless it was possible to know Lamb and yet dislike him quite a lot. For first-hand evidence on this matter we can turn to the preface to *The Last Essays of Elia*, where Lamb, desiring to be rid of his other self, provides an obituary sketch of "the late Elia". Though it is never safe to take Elia's statements for gospel unless there is supporting evidence from another quarter, the germ of truth is no doubt in the following, whatever exaggeration may accompany it: "My late friend was in many respects a singular character. Those who did not like him, hated him; and some, who once liked him, afterwards became his bitterest haters. . . . Few understood him; and I am not certain that at all times he quite understood himself. He too much affected that dangerous figure—irony. He sowed doubtful speeches, and reaped plain, unequivocal hatred." If this was so, we have to remember that he was pursued by many who flocked to him (as P. G. Patmore remarked in the *Court Magazine* after Lamb's death) "from mere idle curiosity, and the excitement of seeing and hearing something different from the ordinary modes of social intercourse", and since it is unlikely that he would conduct himself as a literary lion proper, he may have made enemies from some such cause.

In the same article Patmore put forward the strong theory (which Leigh Hunt said was a grievous error) "that a frequent communion with intellects of the lowest class of cultivation and development was indispensable to the due exercise and the healthful tone of Lamb's mind. . . . Lamb was a king in the realms of intellect; and certain it is that the meanest peasant or vassal of those realms, and even the merest outcast, was deemed by Lamb to come as fairly under the category of 'good company' as the most courtly of lords, the most accomplished of ladies, or the most cultivated of literati". Hunt objected, "it is not intended, surely, to imply by this, that Lamb was fond of the company of outcasts for its own sake, or that he ever 'kept company' with any such people. He did them all justice undoubtedly, and insisted on seeing fair play to the causes of their errors and the amount of their humanity; but to judge from our author's text, it might be supposed that he really had some pet rascals among his friends, and was as fond of them as of anybody! This would occasion a grievous error." So far as we know there were no pet rascals in Lamb's entourage, but (his own words) "he never greatly cared for the society of what are called good people", which is as much as to say that he detested self-righteousness.

CHAPTER FOUR

DOMESTICATION

§ 1

UNDER the shock of Mary's frenzy at the Little
Queen Street lodging, Charles had renounced
love and poetry. At best, he was obviously not
intended by the deity to be either a great lover or a
great poet, though he was destined after an interval
to dally again both with verse and the prospect of
matrimony. But in the meantime—and that meantime was much prolonged—prose and bachelordom
claimed him. "Charles and Mary at home" has
long been a popular theme with devoted Elians,
as it is, indeed, an engaging one for all. They
set up home together (in 1799, after their father's
death) in Chapel Street, Pentonville—at No. 36,
after leaving No. 45 into which the family had first
moved from Holborn. In the next thirty-six years
Charles—sometimes with Mary, sometimes without,
when she was again under restraint—changed his location in turn to Southampton Buildings, Mitre Court,
Inner Temple Lane, Dalston, Great Russell Street
(Covent Garden), Colebrook Cottage at Islington,
Enfield, and Edmonton, with occasional holiday excursions further afield to Cambridge, Oxford, the Lake
District and elsewhere in response to the invitations
of friends.

From a multitude of sources we are able to gather information shedding light upon the appearance, conversation and habit of both brother and sister. It has been a persistent popular error to suppose that Mary was a mere satellite of Charles, receiving his favours and devotion without making any equivalent contribution to the joint account. This of course was not so. The self-sacrifice of Charles was matched, if not more than matched, by that of Mary. She loved him perhaps beyond idolatry, but she was also one of his clear-eyed critics, and she endured much from his foibles and weaknesses. To speak summarily, their experience throughout the years was very like that of any other two people who live in the closest proximity. If any rough generalisation about their differing personalities can be true, it may be fairly safe to suggest that whereas his outlook was in the main a humorous one, hers verged on the tragic. Though her mind was for the most part in the lucid intervals both stable and serene, it is almost inevitable that she should from time to time brood darkly upon the prospect which lay before her. In one such mood she wrote to Sarah Stoddart (November 9 and 14, 1805), "My spirits have been so much hurt by my last illness, that at times, I hardly know what I do. I do not mean to alarm you about myself, or to plead an excuse; but I am very much otherwise than you have always known me. I do not think any one perceives me altered, but I have lost all self-confidence in my own actions, and one cause of my low spirits is, that I never feel satisfied with any thing I do—the perception of not being in a sane state perpetually haunts me." Coleridge was present on an occasion when a fit of insanity came upon her after she had met one of her mother's old friends.

"The next day", wrote Coleridge, "she *smiled* in an ominous way; on Sunday she told her brother that she was getting bad, with great agony. On Tuesday morning she laid hold of me with violent agitation and talked wildly about George Dyer. I told Charles there was not a moment to lose; and I did not lose a moment, but went for a hackney-coach and took her to the private mad-house at Hugsden [Hoxton]. She was quite calm and said it was the best to do so." We are told by other observers, also, that Mary contemplated the onset of these illnesses with astonishing tranquillity, as though she possessed, until the very moment a fit of insanity took complete hold of her, an over-riding faculty of control. When she was in good health she was admired, by intimate friends and casual acquaintances alike, for her sweet disposition, clear understanding, gentle wisdom; her aspect of serenity and peace; her noble-toned and practical mind; and (at the age of seventy) her bright eyes were still full of intelligence and fire. If we did not know of her qualities from external sources we should gather much of them from familiarity with her own letters. She was as fine a letter-writer as Charles himself, lacking his antique touch and lambency of wit, but displaying a kind of surgical penetration into the motives of human behaviour which was outside the range of his peculiar and more specialised sensibility. She could write to a young woman on the eve of marriage to offer advice that a wise matron of long-standing could not have bettered; and, it may be added, Mary was very far from being a queer distempered old maid. Whereas from every point of view Charles was the ideal bachelor, in happier circumstances Mary might well have been an ideal wife. In dealing with her brother she had,

assuredly, to cope with many of the problems of a
long-suffering wife. He was devoted to food, and was
imperious when he came home hungry. He was
restless and self-willed: "I have no power over Charles:
he will do—what he will do." He had dismal moods,
and he indulged them; he had feverish teasing ways.
Like most men he could not bear other people's
toothache patiently; when Mary was slightly out of
sorts he moped abominably; though when she was
really ill he was very good—"good in every sense of
the word, for he has been very kind and patient with
me and I have been a sad trouble to him lately".
Their experience was the common everyday one so
well-known to everyday people: they could surmount
the extraordinary afflictions, but they were frequently
overborne by the fret of daily contacts; "you would
laugh, or you would cry, perhaps both, to see us sit
together, looking at each other with long and rueful
faces, and saying, 'how do you do?' and 'how do you
do?' and then we fall a-crying, and say we will be better
on the morrow. He says we are like toothach and his
friend gum bile, which, though a kind of ease, is but
an uneasy kind of ease, a comfort of rather an uncomfortable sort". But for the most part they were happy
and content together, writing at the same table,
playing cards together, walking in one another's
company, delighting in the same friends, indulging
a mutual passion for snuff, but not reading the same
books, except Shakespeare. It is difficult to find any
unadmirable qualities in Mary, unless it is the sus-
picion of snobbishness which made her dislike any
reference to the fact that Charles had been a clerk;
she could not overcome (said Crabb Robinson) the
instinct to conceal lowness of station. Her insight into

character was remarkable, for although the witnesses are unanimous in registering the impression that she was always gentle and tender to her brother, behaving toward him as an admiring disciple, she could on occasion be caustic in lighting upon his weaknesses— as when—Crabb Robinson having professed himself "highly indebted" to Lamb for useful information on "sundry matters of taste and imagination" while the informant was too tipsy to speak intelligibly—Mary notes ironically that Charles "swallowed the flattery and the spirits as savourily as Robinson did his cold water". Lamb's addiction to the pipe and the bottle were a constant source of distress to Mary. He foreswore tobacco as frequently as Pepys renounced playgoing, and with as little result. In the end tobacco was accepted as an incurable indulgence, but drinking, though equally chronic, was a more serious and less condonable vice. "Charles was drunk last night and drunk the night before"; "Charles brim-full of gin and water and snuff"—such phrases form a recurrent burden in Mary's letters. Callers tell how she watched over him and the bottle. When she objected he would for the moment refrain; but by persistent wheedling would at last prevail. In some recollections written after Lamb's death, P. G. Patmore said, "He would never let you go away from his house, whatever might be the weather or the hour, without walking several miles with you on your road. And his talk was always more free and flowing on these occasions. There was, however, another reason for these walks. In whatever direction they lay, Lamb always saw at the end of them the pleasant vision of a foaming pot of porter. . . . When Lamb was quitting home with you to accompany you part of the way on your journey, you could always see that his sister had rather he stayed at home; and not seldom her last salutation to him on his leaving the room was—'Now, you're not going to drink any ale, Charles?' 'No! No!' was his half impatient reply." Though it is not necessary to lay emphasis upon his liking for alcohol, it is desirable to save him from two opposing classes of people: those who (like Carlyle) see him as nothing better than a sot, and those who will not have it that he was anything worse than a harmless cheerful tippler. Patmore took the improbable line that the artificial stimulus of drink was required to maintain the healthy tone of Lamb's mental condition, and suggested that by "badgering him on this matter of intoxicants Mary kept him from the certainty of being well as much as from the chance of being ill". The niceties of the matter need not detain us; he was what he was, drunk or sober; the indecent thing would be to apologise for him on any pretext. His may have been one of those cases where a too orderly youth was followed by the delayed working-off of high spirits at an age when most of us have settled into a sober solemnity. Some of his ways must have been, to say the least, disconcerting —as when, entering a friend's drawing-room, he could not resist the impulse to play leap-frog over the head of a visitor he happened to notice standing with bent shoulders in the middle of the room. Need we wonder if he was written down by the ponderous Carlyle as a "pitiful, ricketty, gasping, staggering, stammering Tomfool"? To one who was himself mentally drunk with the torrential fluidity of his own lashing eloquence, Lamb's speech-impediment must have been a source of terrific irritation. Others found it a piquant addition to his personal charm, and Lamb

G

himself does not seem to have been greatly distressed by this drawback—and a drawback it was if we are to trust some of the stories told in this connection. There was, for instance, the famous occasion when, Lamb having been recommended to undertake a course of sea-bathing, two beach-attendants at Hastings were commissioned to dip him in the sea. His difficulty in ejecting the word "dipped" caused them to anticipate his instructions and to endeavour to minimise his lingual embarrassment by repeatedly plunging him into the water, before he finally completed the sentence, "I tell you that I am—no, that I *was*—to be di- di-dipped only *once*".

One of the minor mysteries of the relationship between Lamb and his sister is how Mary got him to tolerate her becoming an authoress. Charles had an undisguised detestation of intellectual women, and when once discussing a popular woman writer he said (it may be with only mock ferocity) : "If she belonged to me I would lock her up and feed her on bread and water till she left off writing poetry. A female poet, or a female author of any kind, ranks below an actress I think". We may doubt the seriousness of his remark in view of his affection for the theatre and his frequently declared admiration for the acting profession, admiration which was certainly not confined to male players, since he himself desired to marry one of the foremost actresses of his day. Lamb's real aversion, no doubt, was to that particular type of pretentious female intellectualists comprehensively termed blue-stockings, a type with which Mary was occasionally known to hobnob, as can be gathered from his amusing refer-ences to one of Coleridge's admirers : "I came home t'other day from business, hungry as a hunter, to dinner, with nothing, I am sure, of the *author but hunter* about me and who found I closeted with Mary but . . . one Miss Benje, or Benjey—I don't know how she spells her name. I just came in time enough, I believe, luckily to prevent them from exchanging vows of eternal friendship. It seems she is one of your authoresses, that you first foster, and then upbraid us with. But I forgive you. 'The rogue has given me potions to make me love him.' Well; go she would not nor step a step over our threshold, till we had promised to come and drink tea with her next night. I had never seen her before, and could not tell who the devil it was that was so familiar." Going on to tell Coleridge of his ordeal when they visited Miss Benger (her actual name) Lamb registers the conviction that the knowledgeable female chose to talk on subjects and in a foreign language with which he was unfamiliar, with the deliberate intention of discommoding him and demonstrating her own superior intelligence.

Mary herself at first regarded her projected adventures in authorship as hardly more than vapouring and vapourish schemes floating in her head. This was in 1806, the year in which she was to set to work on the *Tales from Shakespeare*. When these were finished she was more than a trifle puzzled to know what to turn to next. Like her brother, she had little inventive ability, and as a writer she depended upon some structure of fact to provide a starting-point. She told her friend Sarah Stoddart that Charles wanted her to write a play (plays were much in his own head at that juncture, because his farce, *Mr. H.*, had lately been accepted for production, when opportunity occurred, at Drury Lane); but Mary, sensibly, could not see herself as a playwright, and urged Sarah to invent for her some story that could be written up as a child's book or as a novel. That her work, in total, was not voluminous cannot in any way surprise us when allowance is made for the restrictions of time imposed by illness, by caring for Charles, and by helping to entertain the many friends who assembled at the weekly parties which were for a long while a feature of their life together. Charles Lamb was sufficiently the average man to display a definite frigidity toward any departure from the domestic norm of a woman's interests. When the pair moved a second time from the Temple and took up their residence in Great Russell Street, Covent Garden, he informed Dorothy Wordsworth that Mary had not been there for twenty-four hours before she saw a thief. "She sits at the window working, and casually throwing out her eyes, she sees a concourse of people coming this way, with a constable to conduct the solemnity. These little incidents agreeably diversify a female life." Lamb, it would seem, would have preferred the womanly woman to the emancipated female.

Numerous descriptions have been given of the physical appearance of these two, and there is no difficulty in summoning them vividly before the mental eye without the aid of pictorial portraits. Unfortunately, it was not until Charles had achieved some eminence that writers began to set down their impressions of his sister, so that it has become customary for us to think of her almost exclusively as she was in later years. The effect she made was graduated according to the degree of intimacy the describer could claim. To one who saw her for the first time she appeared "a rather shapeless bundle of an old lady, in a bonnet like a mob-cap"; to another, meeting her at breakfast, she seemed a small, bent figure, hard of hearing; to yet another casual observer she "presented the pleasant appearance of a mild, rather stout, and comely maiden lady of middle age. Dressed with Quaker-like simplicity in dove-coloured silk, the transparent kerchief of snow-white muslin folded across her bosom, she at once prepossessed the beholder in her favour, by an aspect of serenity and peace. Her manners were very quiet and gentle, and her voice low". The most taking picture of her is that given by the Cowden Clarkes: "Miss Lamb bore a strong personal resemblance to her brother; being in stature under middle height, possessing well-cut features, and a countenance of singular sweetness, with intelligence. Her brown eyes were soft, yet penetrating; her nose and mouth very shapely; while the general expression was mildness itself. She had a speaking-voice, gentle and persuasive; and her smile was her brother's own—winning in the extreme. . . . Her manner was easy, almost homely, so quiet, unaffected and perfectly unpretending was it. Beneath the sparing talk and retired carriage, few casual observers would have suspected the ample information and large intelligence that lay comprised there. . . . Her apparel was always of the plainest kind; a black stuff or silk gown, made and worn in the simplest fashion. She took snuff liberally—a habit that had evidently grown out of her propensity to sympathise with and share all her brother's tastes; and it certainly had the effect of enhancing her likeness to him. She had a small, white, and delicately-formed hand; and as it hovered above the tortoise-shell box containing the powder so strongly approved by them both, in search of the stimulating pinch, the act seemed yet another link of association between brother and sister."[1] This is a reminiscence by friends who believed a little too heartily in the much canvassed dual-unity of the two, ignoring or perhaps unaware of the fact that is more clearly patent now—that Mary did not sympathise with nor share *all* her brother's tastes and habits; she could, when she would, take a stand of her own and maintain it.

We know the figure of Charles Lamb as well as we do that of Mr. Pickwick, and we should at once be aware of any departure from the authentic portrayal: the short spare figure; the rusty knee-breeches and gaiters; the head and face "black, bony, lean and of a Jew type rather"; the thoughtful forward stoop.

After holding Charles and Mary Lamb together in a willing bondage for so many years Fate was to play a scurvy trick on them in the end. In mutual harmony they had agreed upon the order of their going hence. "You must die first, Mary." . . . "Yes, I must die first, Charles." But while Charles died when still a little under sixty, Mary lived until 1847 (being then eighty-two), surviving him by over twelve years.

§ 2

It has been seen that although Lamb was insistent in his letters that external Nature meant little or nothing to him as compared with the urban contrivances of man, there were outdoor attractions that interested him while he was still a child running about the open spaces of the Metropolis. Skiddaw he professed to despise, in comparison with Fleet Street, yet he was

[1] *Recollections of Writers*, by Charles and Mary Cowden Clarke (Sampson Low, 1878); pp. 177-8.

(for a while) not insusceptible to the attractions of a garden. When they moved to Colebrook Cottage by the New River at Islington, he speaks of the place, with its flowers and fruit and vegetables, as a source of keen delight and was quite taken up with pruning and gardening, finding himself fascinated by such commonplaces as a spider trapping a fly—and that this should have been so is the clearest indication of his previous indifference to the affairs of lesser creatures than men. His strangest departure at this time was the new practice of wearing a flower in his coat. It would be as easy to think of John Knox at a champagne supper as it is to think of Charles Lamb with a buttonhole. Queerly enough, although Lamb would never willingly go into the country to enjoy "the pleasures of nature", he was a great walker. He went on foot to and from the office, walked with Mary frequently in the evening and on Sundays, and on holidays would do his seventeen miles before dinner. An old lady, who remembered Lamb visiting in Hertfordshire toward the end of his life, told Mr. E. V. Lucas that he once walked the twenty-two miles from London to Widford with Emma Isola (the Lambs' adopted daughter). On their arrival Emma was compelled to go to bed for two or three days until her feet recovered from the effects of the long tramp. "Mr. Lamb", this informant added, "often had blisters too, but he did not seem to mind: he loved walking too much." He was sometimes responsible for blisters on Mary's feet also, and she did mind.

We do not know that Charles Lamb had any such tenderly profound consideration for animals as his brother John displayed in an impassioned tract against cruelty to dumb creatures, though it is a little doubtful whether John himself would have left his dinner (as

Charles once did) in order to open the front gate so that a stray donkey might enjoy the quiet comfort of the garden and the more succulent grass within. On another occasion Charles' pride in his staying-power as a walker outweighed those other altruistic instincts, for, according to the Cowden Clarkes, there was a dog who used to follow him when he went out for his daily walk while living at Enfield: "Unendurably teased by the pertinacity of this obtrusive animal, he determined to get rid of him by fairly *tiring him out!* So he took him a circuit of many miles, including several of the loveliest spots round Enfield, coming at last to a by-road with an interminable vista of uphill distance where the dog turned tail, gave the matter up, and lay down beneath a hedge, panting, exhausted, thoroughly worn out and dead beat; while his defeater walked freshly home smiling and triumphant." Over against this heartlessness must be set the knowledge that Charles was more sensitive to the welfare of their own dog, Dash, who appears to have played as many practical jokes upon his master as the master himself would undoubtedly have played if he had chanced to belong to the canine species.

In the end, however, if we would get a true conception of the characteristic and unique Lamb, we must put aside all talk of vegetable and animal nature and come back indoors to eating, drinking, talking, smoking, and card-playing humanity. Lamb in the open air was, almost, a Lamb in fancy dress. He impishly delighted in the poet's phrase about "a party in a parlour, all silent and all damned", but Lamb's parties, whether or not they were damned, were far other than silent. They met at first on Wednesday evenings, later on Thursdays, and, in their last phase, monthly. Nearly everyone who attended them and could write has given some description of the gatherings. The accounts vary but little. There is, naturally, much about them in Crabb Robinson's diary, though he was an habitué who was hardly at home in a company which gave itself largely to whist. But (happily for Robinson) it was not silent whist, as we know from B. W. Procter, whose pen, as well as that of Serjeant Talfourd, provided detailed descriptions of the cold lamb and beef, the veal pies, the hot potatoes, the punch and brandy and porter which sustained and enlivened the guests—and also the host, if not the hostess. Though each of the accounts dwells lengthily upon the eager talk which counted to most of those present for more than cards and physical comfort, it is Hazlitt—in the essay *On the Conversation of Authors*—who has established permanently in literature the "lively skirmishes" at the Lamb's Thursday evenings. After telling something of the impromptu proceedings on those occasions he expresses regret that those days are over: "There is no longer the same set of persons, nor of associations. Lamb does not live where he did. By shifting his abode, his notions seem less fixed. He does not wear his old snuff-coloured coat and breeches. It looks like an alteration in his style. An author and a wit should have a separate costume, a particular cloth: he should present something positive and singular to the mind. . . . Our faith in the religion of letters will not bear to be taken to pieces, and put together again by caprice or accident."

§ 3

Many authors have been sneered at for using their friends as literary copy. No writer ever did this more

consistently than Lamb and none ever earned less
blame for it. His discretion was absolute, and although
George Dyer did once correct a detail or two in one
of the essays referring to himself there was never any
trifle of ungenerous misrepresentation (unless it be of
Charles Lamb himself) from first to last. If it should
happen (God forbid that it should) that Lamb's life
falls into the hands of a film scenario writer we may
expect to be given some episodes concerning "The
women in his life". Leaving Mary out of account,
these were four in number, one of whom—Alice-Anna
—has already been mentioned as his first love. Then
there was Hester Savory. She would be ideal for the
film men as an instance of highly romantic passion,
for though Lamb loved Hester he never spoke to her.
On the screen we could have affecting sequences
showing Lamb following the beautiful Quakeress of
Pentonville at a distance with a hang-dog air, haggard
in languishing hopelessness. Hester was the daughter
of a Quaker goldsmith and lived with her family close
by the Lambs when they were in Chapel Street.
The Savorys' house was the last of a row, a circumstance
which caused Lamb long afterwards to refer to her
as "The Witch of End-door". She married in the
summer of 1802 and died in February 1803. In the
following month Lamb sent to his friend Manning
a copy of the verses beginning "When maidens such as
Hester die", the most beautiful poem which was to
come from the pen of one who, as a poet, was doomed
to fall a good deal short of perfection. Yet *Hester* is an
all-but-perfect poem, and its failure to achieve final
perfection is no doubt due as much to the certainty
that Lamb was incapable of being the perfect lover as
to his shortcomings in the shaping of words into the
forms of poetry.

Lamb was twenty-eight when Hester died, and by the age of forty-three he might have been assumed to be still fancy free, if not indeed of an age when romantic fancy is beyond the likelihood of revival. Yet in truth Lamb had been nursing affectionate longings for some time past in regard to one of the popular actresses of his day, Fanny Kelly. The story of the relations between these two as told in a very few letters, and as revealed by implication in scattered references in Lamb's works, is most creditable to both. The more one reads concerning actresses the greater one's admiration for them is inclined to become. In those instances where they have swum into the ken of literary men they have customarily borne themselves with grace and dignity and held their own on an intellectual level that might be considered beyond their range. Ellen Terry at the end of the nineteenth-century proved herself the equal of Bernard Shaw, as at its beginning Fanny Kelly had caused Charles Lamb to listen with rapt attention to her conversation. And just as Shaw was able to express his admiration for Miss Terry in public tributes as a dramatic critic, so also, though more rarely, was Lamb able to laud Miss Kelly. She was born in 1790 and something is known of her early years through her appearance in the Elia essay *Barbara S——*. There, as usual, a good deal of allowance has to be made for the characteristic mixture of fact and fiction used by Lamb throughout the essays, but if the incidentals concerning this episode in the life of the child actress have been tinctured with fancy the essentials are close enough to accuracy for us to gather that Fanny Kelly had no easy childhood. Elia relates that Barbara's father had practised as an apothecary: "But his practice from causes which I feel my own infirmity too sensibly that way to arraign—or perhaps from that pure infelicity which accompanies some people in their walk through life, and which it is impossible to lay at the door of imprudence—was now reduced to nothing. They were in fact in the very teeth of starvation, when the manager [of the Old Bath Theatre] who knew and respected them in better days, took the little Barbara into his company." The essay, as is well known, goes on to describe how Barbara, who was the sole support of the family, was, one pay-day, accidentally handed a whole guinea instead of half a guinea for her week's work, and how after a conflict between impulse and conscience she returned to the pay-office and notified the error. The actual incident in Fanny Kelly's life was a matter of her mistakenly receiving a dilapidated £2 note and returning it to receive in exchange a brand new note for the correct sum of £1. In spite of the fascination which the theatre exercised over Lamb from childhood to late years, his personal attraction to Fanny Kelly was not due to the glamour of the footlights. If we may judge from independent evidence she was a homely person as well as a fine actress—simple and domesticated as well as one who could rend the heart in the representation of conflicting emotions. Lamb has made her "divine plain face" famous to later generations, and others noted her complete freedom from flamboyance or theatrical pretension when she was off the stage. To Crabb Robinson in 1820 she seemed a young, handsome, agreeable, composed and sensible person; to the same observer in 1828 she was unaffected, clear-headed and warm-hearted. When Miss Kelly was fortyish someone noted that the bloom as of childhood was still on her cheek and that her face was innocent of rouge. We may be sure, considering the vulnerability of actresses, that if there had been any malicious thing to say of her it would not have remained unsaid. In the middle of 1819 Lamb at length brought himself to the sticking-point, and on the 20th of July he sent a letter to little Fanny Kelly suggesting with the utmost tentativeness, yet with a certain resolution, that she should throw in her lot with him (or, rather, "with us" was his phrase) and throw off the burden of her profession. He said with emphasis that he had learned to love her even better off the stage than on, and invited her to think the matter over at her leisure. But she needed no interval for consideration. Her reply reached him on the same day: nothing, she told him, could induce her to change an early and deeply-rooted attachment, but she was sensible of the high honour Lamb's preference conferred upon her. Still on the same day, Lamb's rejoinder was composed, submitting to his rejection as a lover but hoping that Miss Kelly would remain good friends with them and still send them free tickets for the theatre. The hope was justified and the actress remained a good friend and visitor to Charles and Mary, dying still unmarried in 1882 at the age of more than ninety. We might wish on the whole that the proposal had never been made—it was a trifle fantastic that Lamb at forty-four should have wished to marry Fanny at twenty-nine. If his wishes in this respect had been gratified it is possible that he would have appeared a less pathetically lonely figure than some part of posterity has chosen to consider him, but in all probability the pathos would only have been escaped at the cost of tragedy; and the tragedy—or would it merely have been misery?—

is likely to have pressed more heavily upon her than upon him: it would be too romantic to imagine that marriage could have been a satisfactory substitute for tobacco and old books and gin—competitors a wife might less easily tolerate than a sister.

The year following this proposal to Fanny Kelly, the Lambs were on holiday at Cambridge, and at the house of a friend they met a child of eleven named Emma Isola. The girl's mother was dead and her father was an official of the university, with chiefly ceremonial duties to perform. The next we hear of Emma Isola is in a letter written by Lamb to her aunt (Miss Humphreys) in January 1821, in which he tells this correspondent that Emma will be returning to Cambridge on the Wednesday afternoon—he fears somewhat dissipated in appearance but improved in general manners by the company she has recently been keeping. From this it is evident that the Lambs had been entertaining Emma during the Christmas holidays, and Charles assures the aunt that Emma had been a very good girl except for an incurable habit of dog-earing his books and pinching the ears of Pompey their dog. Emma's father died in 1823 and round about that date Emma Isola was taken by Charles and Mary as their adopted daughter. Not much is known about her home life with the Lambs. She was in fact away at school a good deal of the time, and in 1828 she became governess in a Suffolk family. Lamb is recorded to have spoken and written of her variously as "a girl of gold", "a silent brown girl", as of a somewhat pensive cast, and as "the most sensible girl and the best female talker" he had known. He instructed her in arithmetic and both he and Mary did their utmost to teach her Latin, but it has to be concluded that the latter was a task of some considerable difficulty. "I am teaching Emma Latin to qualify her for a superior governess-ship; which we see no prospect of her getting. 'Tis like feeding a child with chopped hay from a spoon. Sisyphus—his labours were as nothing to it"—so Lamb informed Mrs. Shelley. "Actives and passives jostle in her nonsense, till a deponent enters, like Chaos, more to embroil the fray. Her prepositions are suppositions; her conjunctions copulative have no connection in them; her concords disagree; her interjections are purely English 'Ah!' and 'Oh!' with a yawn and a gape in the same tongue; and she herself is a lazy, block-headly supine. As I say to her, Ass *in præsenti* really makes a wise man *in futuro.*" Emma was however duly installed in a governess-ship, and from the letters written by Lamb to her mistress it must be judged that she was extremely happy and kindly treated. A severe illness in 1830 necessitated her return to her adoptive parents. Three years later it became apparent that Edward Moxon the publisher had developed a special interest in Emma, and they married in July 1833, a week after Moxon had given Emma a watch which, so Lamb informed him, had turned her head and made her arrogant and insulting to their old clock in the passage.

It was Lamb's desire to see Emma well married and he had his wish, though her going was none too easy for him to bear. But Lamb was never one to wear his heart on his sleeve in private, and towards the end of the year he asks Moxon to tell Emma "I every day love her more, and miss her less".

CHAPTER FIVE

BOOKS, PICTURES AND THE THEATRE

§ 1

"MIDNIGHT darlings!" When Lamb thus addresses his books it is a little difficult to decide whether he is wearing his heart on his sleeve in public or only writing with his tongue in his cheek. "My midnight darlings, my Folios! must I part with the intense delight of having you (huge armfuls) in my embraces?" The lapse of time has lent a romantic interest to Lamb's home library which it did not always present to those who had inspected his shelves. The phrase "ragged regiment" undeservedly applied by him to his friends, others would have used unhesitatingly for his books. A shudder must run down the spine of sentimental modern book-lovers when they read, in a passage already quoted from one of Mary's letters, how Lamb ransacked his volumes for pictures he could wrench out to fasten on the walls of that bare room they discovered adjoining their own apartments in the Temple. Was it as an act of penance for these violations that on another occasion he raped his walls of their Hogarth prints and, to Mary's mortification at first, had them bound together as a book? The fastidious Crabb Robinson was definitely pained when he saw that Charles' library con-

tained what he described as the finest collection of
shabby books he had ever seen; many of them first-
rate works of genius, he admitted, but so many "filthy
copies, which a delicate man would really hesitate
touching, is I think nowhere to be found". Yet, having
thus aspersed the collection, he remarks blandly that
he borrowed several of the books—though not, we
could guarantee, the filthy ones. Whatever their condition, however, Robinson was repeatedly drawn to
Lamb's shelves and his observations upon the contents
are interesting. We learn from him and from a
younger friend that Lamb threw away all modern
books except those he had liked when a boy—"Trash"
Robinson called those. The "beginnings of two
wretched novels" which he once glanced at while
with the Lambs were, we may be sure, something to
do with Mary, for she was (to Lamb's pretended
disgust) an inveterate novel-reader, and although she
shared some part of his pleasure in gloating over the
precious purchases he made in their lean years, he
failed to convert her to sharing his own whole-hearted
devotion to the antique writers. For a less sophisticated
mind than Crabb Robinson's—that of Thomas Westwood who as a boy lived next door at Enfield—Lamb's
library held many delights. There young Westwood
found Beaumont and Fletcher (of course), Defoe and
Fielding, and that early copy of the *Compleat Angler*
which was to lead Westwood in a direction which made
him a leading authority on the pastime that Izaak
Walton immortalised. Still, Westwood acknowledges
that in outward appearance those shelves presented anything but a tidy appearance; who can wonder?—Lamb's
book-binder at that time was a neighbouring cobbler
who, as Westwood says, patched and botched the

H

volumes without Lamb's perceiving any reason to be dissatisfied with the rough-and-ready handiwork. Had he not remarked, elsewhere, that "in some respects the better a book is, the less it demands from binding"? The truth is that Lamb was not in the nice sense a book collector at all—"book collectors" are, anyhow, the illegitimates of literature. Lamb was something much better: he was a book reader, and it would be interesting as well as vivid to hear his opinion of those collectors of his own MSS. who love him and his work so dearly that they decline to permit the ordinary reader to have access even to a printed transcript of their possessions. There is a touching story which another old friend of the Lambs gave to Mr. E. V. Lucas concerning an occasion when she visited Mary after the death of Charles. The old bookcase was filled with dilapidated books still bearing dealers' labels marked with the prices Lamb had paid long ago. Mary, aged as she was then, led her visitor to the case, "before which we paced up and down, now and then stopping to look at it and even to touch it".

Lamb did not talk a great deal about books in the *Essays of Elia*—for, after all, men and women interested him more than books; but he has left posterity in no doubt as to his opinion of book borrowers, among whom he was himself probably numbered. In *The Two Races of Men* he glances askance at Coleridge's habit of raiding his shelves, leaving foul gaps where previously stood Sir Thomas Browne and Burton and Walton and others not a few. But what a handsome acknowledgment stands in the next paragraph: "One justice I must do my friend, that if he sometimes, like the sea, sweeps away a treasure, at another time, sea-like he throws up as rich an equivalent. . . . I have a small under-collection of this nature (my friend's gatherings in his various calls), picked up he has forgotten at what odd places, and deposited with as little memory at mine. I take in these orphans, the twice deserted."

§ 2

Next to books Lamb loved pictures—not always, perhaps, with a discernment that commends itself to modern preferences; but he had taste in this relation as in most others. We should not now go all the way with him in his enthusiasm for Hogarth—not because we think less of Hogarth's genius than he did, but rather because we now rate Hogarth higher as an artist while thinking him less impressive as a moralist. We are very well acquainted with those Hogarths in narrow black frames which hung on the walls at Inner Temple Lane before they took refuge between book covers. They provided material for discussion at the evening parties, as well as for one of the most perceptive essays written by Lamb under his own name before he became familiar to the world as Elia. He had known Hogarth's two series, *The Harlot's Progress* and *The Rake's Progress*, almost as long as he could remember, for copies hung in the hall of the great silent house in Hertfordshire where he used to stand as a child in speechless interest when staying with grandmother Field. Children are incorrigible moralists, although we in the twentieth century are so foolish as to believe the contrary, and it was because Lamb had so early fallen under the spell of Hogarth as a terrifying teacher that he was ever after incapacitated from judging him in any equivalent degree as an artist. He does in fact say that whereas other pictures can be looked at, Hogarth's are to be *read*. We might anticipate, from this beginning, that Lamb as an art critic would be incapable of judging pictures except as anecdotes in colour or line. And this indeed is largely so. When he confers the palm of superior genius upon Hogarth in comparing *Gin Lane* with Poussin's *Plague of Athens*, he confuses the issue so far as aesthetic considerations are in question by asking us to abstract our minds from the fascination of colour in the French picture and to forget "the coarse execution" of the Hogarth print, in order that we may look without distraction upon the happenings depicted in the two works. It is always what he calls Hogarth's "moral walk" that engages Lamb and hardly ever the craftsmanship; it is *subject*, to the almost entire exclusion of *technique*. If we now differ from Lamb in estimating Hogarth's genius it is because we think of this great English artist as making his masterly effects quite as much through a firm command of his aesthetic medium as through the force of his moral fervour. We see Hogarth, that is to say, as a great artist in the full sense, whereas Lamb saw him as an inspired teacher who happened to be using graphic forms instead of words as the structural basis of his sermons. And in this case it was the sermon that interested Lamb to the virtual exclusion of the structure. It is a great pity for his standing as a naturally qualified though informal art critic that he should have been brought up on Hogarth, for, as we see in the Elia essay on the *Barrenness of the Imaginative Faculty in the Productions of Modern Art*, he had a true notion of what was wrong with the merely anecdotal type of picture which was arriving at a vast popularity in his lifetime. If he had first met Hogarth at a maturer age he would have seen how far that artist's genius transcended whatever sermonising power it embraced. Faced by John Martin's *Belshazzar's Feast* Lamb could estimate immediately the feebleness of an accumulation of anecdotal detail. He realised that what was required was not accumulation but elimination; not a painstaking wonderment of photographic data, but that "wise falsification" by which the great masters of painting reach their "true conclusions". He says, justly, "not all that is optically possible to be seen, is to be shown in every picture". The wise falsification consists in "not showing the actual appearances, that is, all that was to be seen at any given moment by an indifferent eye, but only what the eye might be supposed to see . . . at that eclipsing moment, which reduces confusion to a kind of unity, and when the senses are upturned from their proprieties, when sight and hearing are a feeling only". But here again, the stress he properly lays upon the importance of the imaginative faculty in art is still applied mainly to *subject*, and he appears to have been largely unconscious of the importance of the imaginative faculty in respect of *treatment*. Lamb did not of course bring to art that well informed mind he could bring to literature. Nevertheless there are signs —embryonic perhaps but certain—that he could not have remained indefinitely satisfied with anecdotal pictures and that he would not have submitted without protest to the long tyranny which, after his death, literary interest was to impose upon painting.

§ 3

Taking the objects which provided Lamb with his chief delights, there can be little difficulty or uncertainty in arranging these in the descending order of preference which he would have allotted to them: men and women; theatres; books; pictures.

Some people might take leave to doubt whether it is any part of the function of a godfather to inculcate a love of the theatre in his spiritual charge, but it appears that it was Lamb's godfather Fielde, a Holborn oilman, who must receive the credit or take the blame for introducing Charles to the playhouse. It was he who provided the Lambs with the free tickets which he had secured, not for the first or last time, as an outcome of familiar dealings with members of the Drury Lane Company. Thus first admitted, at the age of five, the boy saw (on December 1, 1780) Arne's opera *Artaxerxes* and a pantomime. He could have remembered little of that evening's entertainment, yet Lamb always regarded it as one of the landmarks of his life, and it laid the foundation of that love of the theatre which continued to be a consuming interest with him until his favourite actors had left the stage nearly half-a-century later. Like his godfather, Charles Lamb delighted in the company of players and had a corresponding interest in free passes. What is less usual, is that the actors regarded him with a more friendly eye than would be cast upon a mere hanger-on. Among them Lamb felt in his natural element, and he used to say—with what accuracy we cannot decide—that he would have been an actor himself but for his stammer. Munden, whose greatness on the stage is almost preserved intact for posterity in Lamb's prose, thought well enough of him to smuggle both Charles and Mary into a corner of the orchestra of a packed house at his own farewell performance. Not only so, but when admirers sent in more pots of stout than Munden could manage, the old actor carried the surplus to Lamb and waited in view of some of the audience to receive the empty measure when it had been obligingly drained by his guest.

Lamb performed two valuable services for the English theatre. He brought the plays of Shakespeare's contemporaries to the knowledge of a larger audience through his critical collection of extracts from their works; and he did as much as can be done to give permanence to a few masterpieces of acting—that most impermanent of all the arts. Though, even in the pages of Elia, they cannot be more than pallid ghosts of themselves, Dodd and Munden and Bensley are vividly re-presented there, and we know something of what they made of their parts. Not only that: we know, too, in what manner Lamb staged the characters on the private stage of his own mind; Iago, by his aid, becomes a credible deceiver; Malvolio an English Don Quixote a little strayed from the perfection of that genius; and, writing of Dodd's performance as Sir Andrew Aguecheek, Lamb does well-nigh succeed in re-creating the whole performance: "You could see the first dawn of an idea stealing slowly over his countenance, climbing up by little and little, with a painful process, till it cleared up at last to the fulness of a twilight conception—its highest meridian. He seemed to keep back his intellect, as some have had the power to retard their pulsation. The ballroom takes less time in filling, than it took to cover the expansion of his broad moony face over all its quarters with expression. A glimmer of understanding would appear in a corner of his eye, and for lack of fuel go out again. A part of his forehead would catch a little intelligence, and be a long time communicating it to the remainder."

So much for the players—but something more for the audience, on the purpose of playgoing. Elia's essay *On the Artificial Comedy of the Last Century* shows how little spectators have changed during a hundred years. Lamb complained, in effect, that the audiences of his day—unlike those of the seventeenth century—took their own world of reality into the theatre with them, expecting the transactions on the stage to bear a colourable likeness to happenings in the everyday world. Later critics were, of course, to complain of the exact opposite—declaring that the theatre presented and its audiences expected only an artificialised and absurdly romantic caricature of life. But Lamb was not concerned with the long-standing antagonism between Realism and Romanticism. His defence of Restoration comedy was based upon the claim that a play may legitimately create its own world, with different terms of being from those which operate in the world of actuality—so that "moral" and "immoral", though valid and indispensable terms in reference to behaviour in the actual world, are without significance when applied to the characters and actions in Congreve's and Wycherley's plays, where a purely phantom world is under inspection and wherein a spectator might reasonably "take an airing beyond the diocese of strict conscience". But Lamb's position, sound enough for himself and a minority of others, can only vainly be pressed upon the multitude. "We dare not dally with images, or names, of wrong. We bark like foolish dogs at shadows. We dread infection from the scenic representation of disaster; and fear a painted pustule. In our anxiety that our morality should not take cold, we wrap it up in a great blanket surtout of precaution against the breeze and sunshine." Lamb was never narrowly logical, and perhaps this theory that there can be one morality for the stage's shows and makebelieve and another for the world at large, does not hold water in face of his own recognition that potencies transport themselves across the footlights and infect the audience, so that, while watching a fine actor or actress, the heart may expand with the desire to perform generous deeds and beat with yearnings of universal sympathy: "You absolutely long to go home, and do some good action." Moreover, that he recognised the power of the stage to corrupt good manners as well as to intensify them is shown by a letter written in September 1801 to William Godwin, in which Lamb comments on a scheme for a play by Godwin. He objects on moral grounds to one proposal, asking if the feeling informing it was likely to be the best sort of feeling: "Is it a feeling to be exposed on theatres to mothers and daughters?" The same question might be asked by a moralist in regard to Restoration comedy. Lamb's reply would no doubt have been that Godwin's proposed historical play had a specific reference to life and should therefore be considered in terms of life and according to living standards, whereas seventeenth-century classical comedy is outside any such frame of reference.

The sympathy we are inclined to expend upon Lamb because fate or circumstance decreed that he should have neither wife nor child, might more appropriately be diverted to condolence over his disappointment-in-chief—his failure to establish successful working relations with the stage, either as actor or as playwright.

CHAPTER SIX

THE LONDONER

§ 1

ADMIRERS of Oscar Wilde's verbal audacities have frequently chuckled over his expression of disappointment on becoming first acquainted with the Atlantic Ocean; but it was forestalled by the best part of a century by Charles Lamb, who reminds us of the still earlier inquiry in Southey's *Gebir:*

Is this the mighty ocean?—is this *all*?

Lamb was a jealous Londoner, and when, while on holiday, he looked upon the mighty works of Nature his impulse was to compare them—to their disadvantage—with his cherished haunts in the metropolis. This may have been an affectation; if so, it was an affectionate one. It is possible, on the contrary, that it was a protest against affectation of another sort —or what could easily seem to be affectation—the ecstatic devotion of Wordsworth and his school to a romantic-philosophic view of Nature. A primrose by a river's brim was perhaps, in private, something more than a primrose to Lamb, but he would have hesitated to admit it in public; and though he was susceptible to the beauty of mountain sunsets he appears to have been relieved when these neglected to live up to their picturesque reputation. He preferred to think of Nature as dead nature. Those majestic presences that it pleased Wordsworth to hail as the garment of God, were to Lamb merely "a house to dwell in". "I must confess", he says to Manning, "that I am not romance-bit about *Nature*." And, again, he consigns "hills, woods, lakes, and mountains to the eternal devil". We know that Wordsworth was almost the only person Lamb regarded with awesome respect as well as affection, but at the same time he does not appear to have acquitted the Lake poet altogether of an inclination to humbug himself through a too-deadly seriousness. Lamb, who did everything with discretion, was a discreet debunker several generations before the Americans invented the word to describe the campaign of moral deflation they undertook with clumsy gusto after the war of 1914 to 1918. It is just as well that Wordsworth did not become infected with Lamb's lively sense of the ludicrous, for some deficiency in the faculty of humorous self-criticism is necessary to a great poet: the sublime becomes the ridiculous when viewed from a slightly different angle. Whatever the cause, however, the urbane need have nothing but gratitude for Lamb's readiness to depreciate Nature, since it moved him to write those magnificent praises of London which appear in letters to his friends. This, to Wordsworth in 1801, is typical: "Separate from the pleasure of your company, I don't much care if I never see a mountain in my life. I have passed all my days in London, until I have formed as many and intense local attachments, as any of you mountaineers can have done with dead nature. The lighted shops of the Strand and Fleet Street, the innumerable trades, tradesmen and customers, coaches, waggons, play-houses, all the bustle and wickedness round about

Covent Garden, the very women of the Town, the watchmen, drunken scenes, rattles,—life awake, if you awake, at all hours of the night, the impossibility of being dull in Fleet Street, the crowds, the very dirt and mud, the sun shining upon houses and pavements, the print shops, the old book stalls, parsons cheap'ning books, coffee houses, steams of soups from kitchens, the pantomimes, London itself a pantomime and a masquerade,—all these things work themselves into my mind and feed me, without a power of satiating me. The wonder of these sights impels me into night walks about her crowded streets, and I often shed tears in the motley Strand from fulness of joy at so much life.—All these emotions must be strange to you. So are your rural emotions to me. But consider, what must I have been doing all my life, not to have lent great portions of my heart with usury to such scenes?" Here, a rural enthusiast might think, is no less (if no more) of humbug than might be suspected in Wordsworth's rhapsodies about mountains and lakes and flowers; but, though that be admitted, it is impossible to know Lamb through his writings without feeling confident that he would have been more capable of sitting in judgment upon his own personal foibles than Wordsworth ever could have been upon his—and that he was in less danger of making confusions between the whisper of his own preferences and the authentic Voice of God. While thinking of Lamb and Wordsworth together, it is a temptation to suggest that the essayist belonged to the eighteenth-century tradition and the poet to the newer age; but the suggestion would have no true relation to the facts. It was not a preference for Nature and a chilliness toward the Town that distinguished the first wave of "the return to Nature" school, so much as a revolt from what these latter believed to be the Popean habit of approaching the phenomena of human existence with staled minds and a set of stereotyped phrases. How far that reading of Pope and his followers was itself erroneous does not at this moment matter. The claim to be made for the Romantics was that they brought fresh and perceptive minds to bear upon phenomena; the question *Town or Country?* was only significant because of the accidental circumstance that the country happened to be the environment in which one of the leading Romantics, Wordsworth, found himself. Their revolt, reduced to essentials, was a revolt from the secondhand; and in this respect Lamb was with the Romantics, though he went to no trouble to wear their mental livery. He would have agreed with Pope that the proper study of mankind is Man—if he could first have been persuaded to agree that there was any *proper* study at all. But Lamb neither saw men through a glass darkly nor as trees walking; he saw them with his own eyes and in their infinitely varied individual shapes. No writer ever took less for granted, or was less inclined to see the human mass as a mass merely. And it was because of his unlimited capacity for differentiation that London was, from beginning to end, his city of delight. But there is no need to think of him as one who was boxed-up in London. While he was no great traveller, the complete tale of Lamb's rural and provincial visitings would fill a long chapter, though not a particularly enthralling one. Except when he went to Oxford and Cambridge and Paris, it was people much more than places which lured him. When he went to the seaside—Margate, Hastings, Brighton —it was rather for Mary's sake than his own, and his comments on Londoners at the sea (in *The Old Margate Hoy*) make strangely up-to-date reading in the twentieth century. There was then, as now, the spectacle of "misses coquetting with the ocean" and the dismal pageant of stockbrokers and their like doing everything in their power to turn the coast into a replica of the places whence they had come, though they made a pretence of escaping with gladness from those places. In the university towns Lamb felt himself in an appropriate setting; there—at one or other—he would have found a comfortable niche if that stammer had not debarred him from fulfilling the obligations and enjoying the privileges of a Grecian's lot. As it was, he had to be content with rare wanderings in Oxford and Cambridge, some memories of which are compacted in the essay *Oxford in the Vacation* and (with more doubtful taste) in *The Gentle Giantess*. In such places as those, Crabb Robinson found it an enjoyment to watch Lamb enjoying himself; and if Charles had no gift for being happy by the sea it was otherwise with Mary, who tells Dorothy Wordsworth: "when I was at Brighton last summer, the first week I never took my eyes off from the sea, not even to look in a book. I had not seen the sea for sixteen years." Said Elia: "We have been dull at Worthing one summer, duller at Brighton another, dullest at Eastbourne a third, and are at this moment doing dreary penance at—Hastings!"—but for "we" in that passage "I" should more correctly be read.

§ 2

The reason for Lamb's impatience with the sea can be found in the virtual certainty that leisure bored him. During most part of his thirty-three years in the East India Company's offices he had yearned to be free from the yoke of day-labour, but scarcely did he gain his heart's desire before freedom began to pall. If he could have been released thirty years earlier to settle to a chosen way of life as an antiquarian and professional man of letters, all might have been well with him so far as his personal comfort was concerned, though it would have been to the disadvantage of literature. Elia was an amateur-of-letters, and his eminence depends utterly upon the good fortune that he was not driven to write for a living; his freshness and originality arise from the happy fact that, in maturity, he had no need to write beyond the scope of his direct experience nor to continue after his best material was used up. Had Lamb in early years made good as a professional journalist there would have been no Elia to undertake the congenial business of recovering from the cellars of memory the slowly mellowed produce of infrequent vintage seasons; he would have been driven by the urgency of journalistic needs to pour them out betimes as raw draughts.

Lamb was within three days of completing his fiftieth year when he applied for permission to retire from service, and his wish was granted less than two months later—on March 29, 1825. The gross amount of his pension was £450 a year, subject to an annual deduction of £9 toward a superannuation grant for Mary Lamb who, after Charles' death, received £120 p.a. from the Company. His net retiring allowance was therefore £441 yearly. In April 1825 Lamb's letters became a song of rejoicing over his release, but it was not long before the tune began to change a little. A few sighs find their way into *The Superannuated Man*, where Elia, recounting visits made to his old colleagues in Leadenhall Street, speaks of feeling himself something of a stranger among those who had been for so long his intimates, though not self-chosen. It seemed at length as if, in those days of unaccustomed leisure, light and power had gone out of him. Literature owes very little to the leisured but much to the enslaved Lamb. After his retirement he wrote one or two essays we would not willingly be without, yet by the end of 1825 the shutters could have been put up without any notable loss to posterity. A Hardy might find grim delight in noting the irony of circumstance which, one year, released Lamb from the torment of regular attendance at an office only to discover him, next year, driven by an inner impulse to journey daily to the British Museum and remain there from 10 to 4 —saying "It is a sort of Office to me—It does me good. Man must have regular occupation, that has been used to it".

In the middle of 1827 another old link was severed by the Lambs' removal from Islington to Enfield. The task of migrating with one's household gods is hateful to all civilised beings, and it was doubly hateful to Charles Lamb with his tendency to sink deep roots into whatever patch of earth supported his domicile. On this occasion as on all such, the incidentals of moving provoked him to an outburst of wry humour on account of women's reluctance to be separated from their familiar junk and clutter. Some years earlier he had written to Manning (March 28, 1809): "I have such a horror of moving, that I would not take a benefice from the King, if I was not indulged with non-residence. What a dislocation of comfort is comprised in that word moving! Such a heap of little nasty things, after you think all is got into the cart: old dredging-boxes, worn-out brushes, gallipots, vials, things that it is impossible the most necessitous person can ever want, but which the women, who preside on these occasions, will not leave behind if it was to save your soul; they'd keep the cart ten minutes to stow in dirty pipes and broken matches, to show their economy. Then you can find nothing you want for many days after you get into your new lodgings. You must comb your hair with your fingers, wash your hands without soap, go about in dirty gaiters. Was I Diogenes, I would not move out of a kilderkin into a hogshead, though the first had nothing but small beer in it, and the second reeked claret."

To move from one part of London to another, or even from the centre to the circumference, might be nothing but a mildly amusing nuisance, but to be transported to the then distant Enfield—to leave the town and decline upon the uncongenial countryside —this was indeed to be uprooted, especially when there followed immediately the added pain of a prolonged recurrence of Mary's mental trouble. Lamb, however, was one of those who could not sojourn in any place without making someone his debtor. Next door to their cottage at Enfield lived the Westwood family, with their boy Thomas, from whose recollections of Lamb some sentences have previously been quoted. Long after Thomas Westwood's death in 1888, his widow—a Belgian—prefaced a small collection of her husband's letters with a brief memoir containing this passage: "My husband had the rare privilege of knowing Charles Lamb when a child, living next door to him at The Chase, Enfield, and of being taken into

I

favour by him. Charles Lamb gave him his first Latin lessons, making them most interesting, and allowed him the free use of his library. Though Mr. Westwood was but a small lad at the time, he fully appreciated this privilege, and he greatly enjoyed his days spent amongst those volumes, his youthful mind grasping their varied contents in a rather surprising manner, which pleased Lamb. He often told me how he used to sit unnoticed under Lamb's table until a late hour in the night, afraid of moving or making a sound lest he should be sent to bed, listening eagerly to the talk of Lamb and his illustrious friends, all those men of genius who assembled nightly in his house. . . . My husband was only eighteen when Lamb died, but in some almost impalpable manner that great man, for whom he had so much reverence and love, left on his manner of thought and his character, a trace through all his life."[1] The accuracy of Mrs. Westwood's impression that the boy received lifelong benefit from his contact with Lamb can be judged from the letters Westwood was writing forty years and more afterward: they are letters with a personal quality that would have delighted Lamb. He resisted many persuasions to write a book on Charles Lamb and was content to print occasional jottings of reminiscence in *Notes and Queries*. The letters to Lady Compton make only passing reference to the Lambs, but enough to show one or two quaint glimpses of Mary—locking up his fishing-rods when the Latin lessons were going poorly, and reproaching him for technical inelegancies in the immature verses he blushingly submitted to her. It is true also that men of genius visited Lamb's house

[1] See *A Literary Friendship:* Letters to Lady Alwyne Compton from Thomas Westwood, 1869–1881 (Murray, 1914); pp. ix–x.

at Enfield, which became a place of pilgrimage for many admirers of Elia, though the boy beneath the table was not likely to distinguish very precisely between the varying qualities of their genius. To Enfield, at any rate, went Wordsworth, Landor, Christopher North, Carlyle, Thomas Hood, Crabb Robinson and others—the influx of visitors scarcely lessened by the greater distance from the centre. Yet a more desperate sense of loneliness and desolation than he had before experienced descended upon Lamb in those years. Mary's recurrent illnesses necessitated her removal for weeks on end, sometimes as far afield as Fulham. His friends were dying in turn or were at a distance, George Dyer had become almost completely blind, and when Lamb made solitary visits to London he felt himself a stranger there: "My old Clubs, that lived so long, and flourished so steadily, are crumbled away. . . . Home have I none . . . and not a sympathising house to turn to in the great city. . . . Yet I tried ten days at a sort of a friend's house, but it was large and straggling—one of the individuals of my old long knot of friends, card players, pleasant companions—that have tumbled to pieces into dust and other things—and I got home on Thursday, convinced that I was better to get home to my hole at Enfield, and hide like a sick cat in my corner." Sometimes, in Mary's absences, forlorn in London lodgings, sometimes staying next door with the Westwoods, Lamb dragged through the days, dreading the prospect of summer because it is devoid of firelight and candles. The brother and sister took a respite from Enfield in 1830 and lodged together for some weeks in Southampton Buildings, Holborn, but the experiment was not a success and they went back. Becoming by stages more

closely acquainted with the Westwoods, Charles and
Mary ultimately went to live under their roof. This
added to the Lambs' disconsolate condition, for their
landlord and landlady (whom they had at first much
liked) proved to be grasping and miserly, and with
great relief Charles informed Wordsworth, in May
1833, that he and his sister were "emancipated from
most *hated* and *detestable* people, the Westwoods". They
had in fact moved to Church Street, Edmonton, and
lived for the short remainder of Lamb's life with
attentive people who kept a sort of small private
asylum—we should nowadays probably describe it as
a nursing-home. There, whatever the disadvantages
in other respects, Charles had the comfort of knowing
that Mary could and would be well cared-for in the
house when the need arose. At that time, the propensity for rambling talk to which Elia affectionately
makes reference as a characteristic of Bridget had
become an almost incessant garrulousness, and for
hour after hour Mary would pour out an unchecked
stream of intermittently coherent chatter about the
past.

One cause of Lamb's rejoicing over the move from
Enfield was that Edmonton is three or four miles
"nearer the Great City". The coaches ran frequently
to London at half the Enfield fare, and of those faci-
lities he intended to avail himself, although so few
friends were by then to be found in town. His
walks at Edmonton were usually on the London road
so that he might imagine himself going to the place
that still held him in bonds. Thomas Westwood (who
did not of course fall under the ban of Lamb's dislike
for the elders at Enfield) wrote: "I believe that,
wherever he might be in the flesh, his life was always

in London—London possessed him wholly. I believe that through the ripple of country leaves and the green reaches of down and meadow he had constant knowledge of the thronged thoroughfares, heard always an echo of the hum and hubbub of the busy streets."[1] And when young Westwood caught the last glimpse of him leaving Enfield, Lamb was walking beside an open cart laden with books—his face towards London.[2]

As Charles Lamb set out for his usual morning walk on December 22, 1834, he stumbled against a stone and fell, grazing his face . . . still turned towards London. . . . The mishap occurred on a Monday, and by Friday evening, erysipelas having set in, he was seriously ill. When Talfourd, in response to a summons, visited Edmonton, on the next morning (Saturday), he found Charles weak in body and wandering in mind, murmuring the names of old familiar friends. There seemed no immediate danger, but within an hour of Talfourd's departure Lamb sank and gently faded out of life.

[1] *Notes and Queries:* May 20, 1882; p. 381.
[2] Ibid., November 23, 1872; p. 406.

PART TWO

THE WRITER

CHAPTER SEVEN

CALENDAR OF WORKS

§ 1

IF Charles Lamb had died on his forty-fifth birth-
day his position in English literature would be
very different from what it now is. Up to the
beginning of 1820 he had written nothing that would
make him appear more important than any of the
minor writers of prose and verse in the Regency period.
There are so few instances in literary history of a man
establishing a great reputation upon work completed
within so short a space of time that it is worth while
surveying, at this point, the work done by Lamb
before he began to use the signature *Elia*; and it is
profitable, too, to note that he not only began his true
work late but also completed it some time before his
death. If the five years from 1820 to 1825 could be
removed bodily from Lamb's record, his ranking would
be definitely below Hazlitt's and certainly no higher
than that of Leigh Hunt, who would in fact have an
advantage inasmuch as Lamb made no such contribution to contemporary political history as Hunt
did.

The earliest surviving example of Lamb's writings
is the poem in a manuscript book kept by James Boyer
the senior master at Christ's Hospital while Lamb was

a pupil there. This set of verses, entitled *Mille Viæ Mortis* is dated 1789 and therefore belongs to the author's fourteenth or fifteenth year. It is known that he was philandering with poetry at the time of Mary's fatal frenzy in 1796, and following that crucial event he determined, as we have seen, to destroy his MSS. and abandon authorship. That determination did not, in the natural course of things, last for more than a relatively few weeks. In the same year Coleridge's *Poems on Various Subjects* appeared, and to this collection Lamb contributed a few sonnets—one addressed to Mrs. Siddons; others to Anna; and one on the pleasures of dispersal in death. Until 1818 Lamb published no poems except those included in volumes by Coleridge and Charles Lloyd, and the only poem of real merit by him up to that date was *The Old Familiar Faces*, printed in the 1798 volume, *Blank Verse* by Charles Lloyd and Charles Lamb. Concurrently, Lamb was experimenting with drama and prose fiction, and his first work of any particular note was *Rosamund Gray*, a short tale published in 1798. It would be as useless as it would be insincere to pretend that these early writings have a high intrinsic value in addition to their interest as part of the rough foundation upon which the later work of Elia was to stand. Although there is nothing of the true spirit of Elia in *Rosamund Gray* the skeleton is there. That is to say, in his first attempt at creative prose he was obviously falling back, as he invariably did afterward, upon autobiographical aids.

Leaving aside for a while such other works in book form as he was to produce during the next twenty years, an account of his early journalistic endeavours is in place here. From first to last, Lamb contributed to some score of newspapers and periodicals, including

the most famous of them all so far as he was concerned
—the *London Magazine*. He had been an occasional
contributor to the press for more than eighteen years,
however, before time and opportunity and experience
coincided to bring him fame through the medium
of a wedding of journalism with literature. It is possible
that if Lamb had been a free agent at the time he
reached his middle 'twenties he would have risked
embarking upon a journalist career rather than submit
to the irksome routine of his clerkship at the East India
House. But the sheet-anchor of his life—Mary's necessity and his devotion to her—prevented his taking
any such plunge; and so far as we can judge from
the extant specimens of his early journalism it is
unlikely that he would have made rapid headway in
a free-lance capacity. It is true that his principal early
spare-time journalistic enterprise was in one of the most
discouraging departments of the *Morning Post*, after
he had had some connection with a moribund weekly
called *The Albion*. Apart from a few fragments of
dramatic criticism, Lamb's contributions to the *Morning
Post* chiefly comprised a daily ration of jokes (then a
popular feature of the London papers), for which he
was paid at the rate of sixpence each for paragraphs
not exceeding seven lines. He has told something of
the difficulties imposed by this pursuit of topical
humour in the Elia essay on *Newspapers Thirty-five
Years Ago*, but the shortage of subjects to which he
refers as the major difficulty probably was not in truth
the main cause of his lack of success. Jokes and puns
were, as all the world knows, as much a part of Lamb's
natural equipment as his stammer; yet, as the world
knows less well, an unbridged gulf separates oral jokes
from written ones. There is every reason for us to

believe that his addiction to the oral form must have
been one of Lamb's most tiresome characteristics,
though this was perhaps a form of facetiousness less
detested a century ago than now. When one knew the
man intimately it was no doubt possible, if not to
enjoy, at least to overlook or endure his persistent
antics as a domestic jokester. But puns and verbal
jokes on a similar low level cannot with effect be
transferred to the printed page, and those examples
of Lamb's *Morning Post* wit which Mr. E. V. Lucas
has salvaged would cut but a poor figure if they should
be matched alongside such instances of witty brevity
as now appear on the weekly Charivaria page of
Punch or in Beachcomber's morning column in the
Daily Express. Lamb himself remarked in this connection that "to swallow six cross-buns daily con-
secutively for a fortnight would surfeit the stoutest
digestion. But to have to furnish as many jokes daily,
and that not for a fortnight, but for a long twelve-
month, as we were constrained to do, was a little
harder execution. . . . No Egyptian task-master ever
devised a slavery like to that, our slavery. No fractious
operants ever turned out for half the tyranny, which
this necessity exercised upon us. Half a dozen jests in
a day (bating Sundays too), why, it seems nothing!
we make twice the number every day in our lives as
a matter of course, and claim no Sabbatical exemp-
tions. But then they come into our head. But when
the head has to go out to them—when the mountain
must go to Mahomet——" There was a rather curious
dichotomy in Lamb in this respect. He was boisterously
humorous as a man, yet most delicately so as a writer.
His example brings us face to face once more with
those notorious difficulties of classification which arise

whenever the nature and sub-divisions of humour are in question. Lamb provided what was possibly the only instance that can be cited of the presence of the broad grin and thoughtful laughter in two sharply separated departments of the one person. Put amid a party of other human beings he could be relied upon to hunt the broad grin with painstaking perseverance; but sit him at a table and put a pen in his hand and the whole character and direction of his humorous pursuit was instantly changed. The two essentials in Lamb's truly characteristic writings are meditative quietness and intimacy, and neither of these is much in request for the purposes of a joke column in the daily press.

Better fortune was to come for Lamb when John Hunt founded *The Reflector* in 1810, with his brother Leigh Hunt as editor. To turn back to those hundred-year-old periodicals is to be reminded how much less formal and how much more leisurely literary journalism was in the early nineteenth-century than today. Editorial lapses were commonplace: serial contributions began but in some cases were either not continued or never ended; publication tended to be irregular; editors took subscribers into their confidence with a paternal or brotherly familiarity—occasionally to excuse their own lackadaisical methods; and if anonymity was more frequent than now, it was a veil that might be lifted at any moment when editor or contributor desired to buttonhole the reader for the purpose of familiar discourse. *The Reflector* was a short-lived quarterly which ceased little more than twelve months after it was born. Nevertheless, it had distinguished contributors, and the Hunts gave Lamb an opportunity similar to that he was to have again a decade later. The interesting problem that arises in connection with Lamb and *The Reflector* is to speculate upon the question of why the success he achieved in the *London Magazine* in 1820 did not come ten years earlier in *The Reflector*. No more restrictions were laid upon him in the first instance than in the second, and if it was a necessary condition for the full exercise of his genius that he should write either anonymously or pseudonymously there is no reason why he should not have chosen his own method of personal projection in the pages of *The Reflector* where he did, in fact, use various pen-names. Within the space of four numbers of this quarterly, Lamb published some ten substantial pieces of prose which are, all the while, hovering on the edge of complete success without ever claiming it with the indisputable certainty that was patent from the first in the Elia essays. More will be said of the content of these contributions later; here it is enough to cite one or two of the titles as an indication of the fancy Lamb was then exercising in a tentative flight: *On the Inconveniences Resulting from Being Hanged, On the Danger of Confounding Moral with Personal Deformity, On the Custom of Hissing at the Theatres, The Good Clerk, A Character.* In irregular succession to his work for Hunt's periodical there followed contributions of no very special merit or importance to such publications as *The Gentlemen's Magazine, The Philanthropist, The Examiner, The Quarterly Review, The Champion, The New Times,* and *The Indicator.* The last named brings us to 1820, when Lamb began to write for the *London Magazine.*

Though Lamb was no politician, politics in the eighteen-tens was too continuously in the air for even the least politically-minded altogether to escape some

slight infection by the passions then raging, chiefly
round the bulky personality of the Prince Regent.
In retrospect it is almost impossible to regard the
Regent as anything more portentous than the puppet-
in-chief in a wild extravaganza, and now that we are
more polite to our own unfantastic royalties. it all
appears as part of the same incredible masquerade
when we read that the deputy monarch was hissed
and stoned in the London streets. But a true sense of
historical perspective compels us to put him in his
proper setting against a national background of wide-
spread want and distress, and when he is viewed in
that relation he can be seen in a truer light as a vicious
swollen popinjay. In Leigh Hunt's paper *The Examiner*
for March 15, 1812—Lamb had a poem entitled *The
Triumph of the Whale* which, after roundly abusing
"the whale" and his entourage—

> Flat fish are his courtiers chief.
> Last and lowest in his train,
> Ink-fish (libellers of the main)
> Their black liquor shed in spite:
> (Such on earth the things *that write*)—

sums up thus:

> Name or title what has he?
> Is he Regent of the Sea?
> From this difficulty free us,
> Buffon, Banks or sage Linnæus.
> With his wondrous attributes
> Say what appellation suits.
> By his bulk, and by his size,
> By his oily qualities,
> This (or else my eyesight fails),
> This should be the PRINCE OF WHALES.

This lampoon was but one of many which *The Examiner* and other papers launched so contemptuously against the "first gentleman in Europe" that they scarcely troubled to employ the conventional indirect methods of satire. But audacity did not make them immune from political penalties. In the issue of *The Examiner* for March 22nd in the same year a more virulent prose attack on the Regent exhausted the patience of the authorities. John and Leigh Hunt underwent, in consequence, the two years' imprisonment which, to students of early nineteenth-century literature, is familiar from the fact that Leigh Hunt, being subjected to little more than preventive detention, furnished his room in the prison infirmary in almost palatial style, surrounded by his family and friends and enjoying the delights of the garden he made.

As Lamb's contributions to the *London Magazine*, though part of his journalistic career, form a separate major episode, the survey of his miscellaneous works published in book form up to that year may conveniently be resumed.

§ 2

The tragedy, *John Woodvil*, started in 1797–8, reached publication in 1802, when it was bound up with a few odd fragments of prose and verse also by Lamb. This first of his dramatic works had a less exciting history than the farce, *Mr. H.*, which succeeded it in 1806. *John Woodvil* could be neglected in any biographical or critical record of Lamb and his work without leaving the slightest hole in the fabric, but it is not so with *Mr. H.* In saying this there is no intention of determining the comparative merit or defects of the two plays, for this is not at the moment under examination. The importance of *Mr. H.* in the canon of Lamb's works depends upon the fact that on the morning of December 11, 1806, Lamb was a different person from what he had been in the early evening of the previous day. On December 10, 1806, *Mr. H.* was produced at Drury Lane with one of Lamb's best-loved actors, Elliston, heading the cast. This was a great occasion in the history of Lamb and his intimates. Charles (of course) and Mary were there, their brother John also; Crabb Robinson and Hazlitt and a posse of Charles' colleagues from the office. It would hardly be possible to overestimate the potential importance of those few hours in Lamb's life, either for himself or for literature. The incidents of the evening do not call for detailed description; it is enough to say that after a promising beginning, when the prologue was warmly received, the audience proceeded to damn the play as unmistakably as the most hopeless of untried dramatists could dread. This blow was the more desolating to Lamb because there is no room to doubt that he had built very high hopes upon the possibility of the play's success, and, so far as can now be gathered, there seems as little doubt that he not only hoped but also expected the reception of *Mr. H.* to be favourable enough to justify his continuing as a playwright. *Mr. H.* is certainly not a good play, but neither is it a shockingly bad one when read alongside many of the pieces which secured popular success round about that period. Its total failure was to some extent due to precipitancy. The preparations for the performance had been hurried and the performance itself failed to do justice to whatever qualities the play possessed. Lamb was precipitate

K

too. The Drury Lane management was prepared to give *Mr. H.* another chance by continuing the run—indeed the management appears to have had some notion that *Mr. H.* pleased the spectators, notwithstanding the cordiality with which they hissed—but Lamb insisted that no second performance should be attempted. In receiving the play as it did, that Drury Lane audience damned more than *Mr. H.* alone; it damned some of Lamb's most cherished hopes and desires. He accepted the verdict as though it were given with the awful finality of an infallible and godlike Parnassian assembly. While it is true that his playwriting experiments did not end with *Mr. H.* he was never again to seek the suffrages of the many-headed. Can it be that some perverse imp always at Lamb's elbow persuaded him that it was preferable to be damned out-and-out than to be half-damned with the possibility of being wholly damned at a second attempt? Or was it that failure was a more fertile subject for wryly humorous meditation in letters and essays than success could have been? The incident was not without its compensations either for Lamb or for posterity. Thereafter, *Mr. H.* incarnated as Elliston became one of the author's cherished friends; and we can recapture the emotions and sensations of the evening through Lamb's own writings and also through the account given in one of Hazlitt's essays. Lamb's behaviour as a member of the audience was thoroughly in character. Hazlitt tells us that Lamb was roaring with laughter at his own wit during the successful prologue, and we know that when the mood changed and the audience hissed, he hissed also.

Referring in an earlier chapter to Lamb's association with William Godwin, we have seen that after Godwin's

second marriage a number of his friends were alienated
by the new Mrs. Godwin's plainly-shown dislike. But
in spite of Lamb's animosity toward her on this and
other counts, she was to be important in the lives of
Charles and Mary. In 1805 the Godwins started a
publishing house which specialised in the issue of
children's books. After Charles had written for the
new venture a set of verses to accompany pictures by
another hand in a booklet entitled *The King and Queen
of Hearts*, Mary set to work upon a project that came
to fruition as the collection of *Tales from Shakespeare*,
which kept the names of Charles and Mary Lamb
alive in the nurseries of the world for at least a hundred years. Only in the present generation has the
repute of that book suffered a serious decline, under
the influence of a new scholastic conviction that paraphrased and pemmicanised classics are a hindrance
more than an aid to literary appreciation. Children
must nowadays take their Shakespeare without crutches
supplied by the Lambs or any other; yet when the
last educational theory goes down abashed into the
womb of eternity there may still be a plea to make
on behalf of Lambs' *Tales from Shakespeare*, published
in 1807. Whatever shortcomings the book may appear
to have from the austere present-day angle, there is
at least one favourable thing that can be said of it:
it is not mawkish—an apparently negative merit which
was in truth a positive quality of the first importance
in an age notorious for the namby-pamby purveyed
by popular writers for children. In the fascinating
history of children's books the Lambs must be credited
with establishing a new and desirable mode, for though
in the introduction to the *Tales* the adaptors hoped
that their transcriptions might become "enrichers of

the fancy, strengtheners of virtue, a withdrawing from all selfish and mercenary thoughts, a lesson of all sweet and honourable thoughts and actions", they were too honest to follow the current fashion of endeavouring to inculcate virtues by methods which made so many contemporary juvenile books appear both half-witted and wholly insincere. The *Tales from Shakespeare* are not, of course, a substitute for Shakespeare; and it is possible that children in the past, having read them, frequently took Shakespeare for granted for the rest of their lives; but nevertheless, it may be better to have Lamb with Shakespeare sauce than not to have either Shakespeare or Lamb at all.

Charles Lamb's next undertakings were, first, another book for children, *The Adventures of Ulysses*, and then the *Specimens of English Dramatic Poets who Lived about the Time of Shakespeare*—both published in 1808. His attempt to do for some part of Homer what had already been done for Shakespeare did not receive an equal degree of popular success, but parents who wish to introduce young children to Greek stories might do much worse than put Lamb's *Ulysses* on the nursery shelves.

In 1809 the Lambs collaborated in *Mrs. Leicester's School* and *Poetry for Children*; and in 1811 Charles issued (again through Godwin) a rhymed children's story from the French, *Prince Dorus*. With these three, their writings for children concluded.

The *Dramatic Specimens* suffers today because of a prevalent inability on the part of modern readers to consider it in relation to its own time. Not more than a handful of people, if so many as that, would now think of approaching the older dramatists by way of Lamb, yet we must do him the justice of recognising that he opened the door to what was then, to all intents and purposes, a locked room. The further question of his critical ability is an altogether different matter, though, before dismissing the high claims that have been made for him in this connection, it has to be remembered that current opinion about Lamb as a critic is still so sharply divided that the lay reader can, according to his preference, accept Lamb either as one of the most genuinely inspired and original-minded of English critics or, on the other hand, dismiss him as an interloper devoid of critical intelligence, taste and judgment.

Anyone who nowadays picks up *The Works of Charles Lamb*, published in two volumes in 1818, can hardly avoid regarding it as a bleak and unsatisfying collection, for it is a strange experience on opening these *Works* (with their title suggesting the completed output of a lifetime) to find none of the writings which have made Lamb a delight to intervening generations. At most, the ordinary reader would desire to retain from these volumes two or three poems and perhaps half-a-dozen prose pieces. In the light of after-knowledge, *The Works of Charles Lamb* is more interesting as a literary curiosity than for any definite attraction in its contents; and the curiosity is made still more curious when we reflect that Lamb himself would almost certainly have dismissed it as the wildest of wild improbabilities if, after the publication of those two volumes in 1818, anyone had suggested to him that he would secure lasting fame without the slightest aid from anything included in his *Works*.

Except *Elia* (1823) and the *Last Essays of Elia* (1833) the only other volume by Lamb published in England in his lifetime was the 1830 volume, *Album Verses*.

Young ladies and others then kept albums in much the same way as their twentieth-century counterparts keep autograph books, but the earlier hobby was a more ambitious one because original verse was demanded and not merely signatures. Lamb was helpful in the matter of Emma Isola's album, as we know from the letters he wrote to his literary acquaintances, begging poems for her, and he himself composed verses for the albums of others. Although the title no doubt had a topical appeal, *Album Verses* was too trivial a designation for Lamb's volume, which contained at least two poems that rank among his best —*On an Infant Dying as Soon as Born* and *The Gipsy's Malison*.

§ 3

In January 1820 the first number of the *London Magazine* came out. It was founded by the firm of Baldwin, Cradock and Joy and edited by John Scott. In the course of its unsteady existence the *London Magazine* had an imposing list of contributors, but it would not stand out with special prominence from the rut of contemporary periodicals if it were not for Lamb's appearance among its authors. The magazine had more ill-hap than good fortune, for Scott (an editor of exceptional ability) disappeared from the scene early in 1821 after being fatally wounded in a duel. This was only a few months after Lamb's first contribution was printed. In August 1821 Taylor and Hessey became the proprietors, and John Taylor took over the editorial charge. The fluctuating fortunes of the magazine during the next few years form an interesting sub-section in the history of English journalism, which it is not necessary to follow here beyond noting that the increasing inaptitude of the managers of the *London* undermined the enthusiasm of its contributors, although Lamb continued to write in its pages—with some intervals and with diminishing interest—until the later part of 1825. To turn over the century-old discoloured pages of the *London Magazine*, and to note their close-set type-area, is to feel a warm admiration for the readers who recognised so readily the genius of the most eminent member of the team. The writers were aided by none of the arts of typographical display that now make literary matter as easily digestible as American breakfast foods, and so far as physical appearance is concerned a common greyness smothers everything in the composition of the *London Magazine*.

When Lamb was requested to write for it, with a free hand to choose his own topics and method of treatment, he appears to have selected his first subject before thinking of the even more famous signature appended to it. He produced the essay on *The South Sea House* and then felt that some of the intimacies in it might not altogether please his brother John Lamb who held a responsible position on the staff of the South Sea Company. Charles accordingly took refuge in a pseudonym, choosing the name of an old Italian scrivener he had known as a colleague while working there as a boy thirty years earlier. Some eighteen months after filching Elia's good name, Lamb went to call upon him—only to find that he had died several months before. In a letter to Taylor, the publisher and editor, Lamb, remarking upon this, adds, "So the name has fairly devolved to me, I think; and 'tis all he has left me." The circumstances as here very briefly cited provoke interesting reflections concerning Lamb and his writing methods. When reading over the paper on *The South Sea House* and feeling that John Lamb might not relish some of the phrases anatomising the place and its occupants, two courses were open. He could have revised the essay, hardening its outlines and diminishing the familiar manner of treatment; or he could have veiled himself (as he actually did) in the personality of another, thus setting himself free from the necessity of adopting a detached attitude. In this way he hit upon the accent which exactly suited his hitherto latent or only half-expressed genius. In the past, his contributions to periodicals had been signed with various pseudonyms, and there seems no reason why he should not completely have found himself at a much earlier date. An analysis of his style and methods at particular stages in his writing life is given later, and it therefore suffices to say here that while writing for the *London Magazine* in 1820 he discovered that it was an imperative necessity for him to utilise the resources of memory as a literary solvent. He could make nothing of raw and indigested material. Without devising any pretentious technical theory— such as that used, with a bow of acknowledgment to English sources, by Proust—Lamb found that his power lay in capturing, for the printed page, remembrances of things past. That he consciously employed technique devices cannot be doubted; there is an artful artifice in every one of his mature sentences—an artifice that was perhaps by that time second nature. In summoning up his recollections of the past, Lamb was aided by his own saturation in the literary manner of a still more remote past. Thomas Westwood insisted that "Charles Lamb was a living anachronism—a seven-teenth-century man, mislaid and brought to light two hundred years too late. Never did author less belong to what was, nominally, his own time; he could neither sympathise with it, nor comprehend it".[1] We may take leave to think that Westwood, in that passage, was laying bare a half-truth only. It seems more likely that Lamb comprehended his own time very well indeed, and that where his sympathies were imperfect they were so with full intent, and not through lack of comprehension. It would be more nearly true to say that Lamb was an early nineteenth-century man sharing the interests of his contemporaries, but bringing to bear upon those interests the apparatus of a seventeenth-century mind. Or, in an alternative interpretation, we might speak of him—using modern jargon—as an escapist. The terms "optimist" and "pessimist" applied to men and women are as absurd as any that could be used, for every civilised being is both optimist and pessimist. Lamb was both. It is tendentious nonsense to think of him as radiating a uniform brightness. The whole gravamen of Southey's very moderate objection to the first Elia volume was based upon the contention that Lamb had shown himself to be pessimistically irreligious. If he had been wholly a pessimist there would be no difficulty in assigning adequate reasons for his pessimism. There was an occasion—no doubt more than one—when he spoke of himself in words as black and bitter as Hamlet's "I could accuse me of such things that it were better my mother had not borne me", and though we may feel that, in Lamb's case, such self-accusations fall into the same category as St. Paul's allusion to himself as the chief of sinners, it is nevertheless proper to remember that Lamb was not the unvarying apostle

[1] *Notes and Queries*, September 22, 1866; p. 222.

of cheerfulness he has popularly been supposed. If by becoming Elia he was able to find relief from the burden of being Charles Lamb, he had better reason for his escapism than can be credited to other writers whose romantic fantasies provide a measure of their reluctance to confront the actualities of life with courage and endurance. There is not the slightest doubt that Lamb was frequently a burden to himself and that he descended now and again into an avernus of hopelessness—especially at those times when Mary's absences thrust upon him an intense experience of loneliness, aggravated by his own sense of failure. Even *Elia* brought him no material success—its vast fame is exclusively posthumous—and he was scarcely exaggerating when he declared "I never had any luck with anything my name was put to", and (as late as 1831) "Nothing with my name will sell, a blast is upon it".

But the blessed word Elia was of enormous importance for Lamb. It did enable him to put into permanent word-form many of those reflections, both the humorous and the half-tragic, which had been simmering inside him for years. The cloak of Elia provided him with a confessional, and, like any form of confessional for any one, it cleansed his bosom of much perilous stuff and, in the process of discharge, there came out also that suffusion of sweetness and light which was inseparably mingled with the bitterer elements. If we ask in this connection why it was that the earlier pen-names had failed to be correspondingly effective, the answer must be found in the fact that, on the hither side of middle age, the assimilating and clarifying influences of memory had been too immature to exercise the requisite potency.

CHAPTER EIGHT

POET AND DRAMATIST

§ I

OUT of every thousand readers who saturate themselves in the *Essays of Elia*, probably less than one troubles to read steadily through Lamb's poems. While the resulting loss of pleasure is small—Lamb is never exciting as a poet, and all true poetry is exciting—there is a considerable amount of interest to be had from asking why it is that his verse always misses poetic excellence even when, once or twice, it comes near to reaching it. The obvious answer is that Charles Lamb had not a first-class mind, in the sense in which great poets have first-class minds. He could not put fine original thought and fine original feeling into fine original language carved into a fine original shape. It has been said that great poets are able to make great poetry out of commonplace material. That is true, in so far as by "commonplace material" is meant such verities of human experience as love, birth, death, and the interplay of these. But, even so, every great poet encounters his commonplaces as though no one in the history of mankind had ever encountered them before, and on his tongue the commonplaces become once more originalities as they were at the dawn of the world.

Whether we call them commonplaces or eternal verities, these are frequently the subject matter of Lamb's verse, but they are not turned into first-rate poetry, because intensity of emotion is never once matched with an intensely personal manner of expression: he does not find the one perfect mould, and hardly ever lights upon the miraculous right word or a line which it is impossible to imagine bettered by revision. In a sonnet to his brother, Charles says

>   'Tis man's worst deed
> To let the "things that have been" run to waste,
> And in the unmeaning present sink the past:
> In whose dim glass even now I faintly read
> Old buried forms . . .

Taking this as text, and remembering that his prose was written "for antiquity", we might explain the non-success of Lamb's poetry by the theory that it is full of echoes, and say that it falls short of vital originality because of an excessive devotion to old buried forms. That would be a simple and possibly a completely satisfying explanation—only it would be far from true. Lamb's verse does echo the tones of greater poets' work, yet the simplicity of that discovery fades when we realise that the echoes are as often echoes of the future as of the past—a paradox equivalent to saying that if Lamb sometimes seems to be writing verse in the manner of Gray's and Collins' odes and Scott's shorter narrative pieces, and sometimes in two other distinct manners caught, no doubt, from Coleridge and Wordsworth, he also writes at single moments (in 1795) like Tennyson before Tennyson was born and (in 1794 and 1795) like Shelley and Keats while they were hardly more than born. We need not hail Lamb as a neglected forerunner of the younger Romantics, for these "echoes of the future" may denote only that the spirit of the age was waking faintly and prematurely in him before it worked with timely and sustained vigour in Shelley and the rest. If it were not that the latest possible date of composition is fixed by their publication in 1796 (when they formed a section under Lamb's name in the volume containing Coleridge's *Poems on Various Subjects*), only a slight exercise of the literary detective instinct would be needed for tracing some pale influence from *La Belle Dame Sans Merci* upon

> Was it some sweet device of Faery
> That mocked my steps with many a lonely glade,
> And fancied wanderings with a fair-hair'd maid?

or a touch of Shelley in

> For now to my raised mind
> On wings of winds comes wild-eyed Phantasy,
> And her rude visions give severe delight.
> O winged bark! how swift along the night
> Pass'd thy proud keel! nor shall I let go by
> Lightly of that drear hour the memory,
> When wet and chilly on thy deck I stood,
> Unbonnetted, and gazed upon the flood,
> Even till it seemed a pleasant thing to die . . .

or to discern in

> Methinks how dainty sweet it were, reclin'd
> Beneath the vast out-stretching branches high
> Of some old wood, in careless sort to lie,
> Nor of the busier scenes we left behind
> Aught envying . . .

a domesticated plagiarism of Tennyson's

> How sweet it were, hearing the downward stream,
> With half-shut eyes ever to seem
> Falling asleep in a half-dream!
>
> .   .   .   .   .
>
> Only to hear and see the far-off sparkling brine,
> Only to hear were sweet, stretch'd out beneath the pine,
>
> .   .   .   .   .
>
> In the hollow Lotus-land to live and lie reclined
> On the hills like gods together, careless of mankind.

As soon as the curious interest of such slight fore-shadowings has been observed, a second glance at these passages from Lamb's verse is enough to show that verbal infelicity would have been his crucial weakness even if there were not invariably also a thinness of content. He could bring a whole poem shattering down by the use of a single ill-chosen word. Thus, in one of the lines quoted above—

> When wet and chilly on thy deck I stood

"chilly" is disastrous, yet it could have been avoided with a moment's labour—

> When chilled and wet upon thy deck I stood.

In another poem (*Hester*), where it is clear that Lamb had given painstaking attention to technique and structure, there is a similar fatal lapse:

> A month or more hath she been dead,
> Yet cannot I by force be led
> To think upon the wormy bed,
> And her together.

Nothing but the controlled emotion and the metrical unity by which the poem is otherwise distinguished prevents *Hester* from being plunged into incurable bathos by the phrase "wormy bed". Reader, said Lamb, "I have no ear". This deficiency is evident in nearly all his poems, and it is significant that *The Old Familiar Faces*, which touches as high a level as any he wrote, is in free verse, and is therefore dependent upon rhythm and not upon metre or music. The failure of his ear can be illustrated further by reference to the verses headed *Hypochondriacus*, where he attempts the kind of poetry that depends upon the use of proper nouns and other words with a ritualistic sound. The concluding lines given below obviously do not invite comparison with the Miltonic manner, but they do form a parallel with the metrical word-patterns that Edgar Allan Poe and Christina Rossetti and one or two others could turn into vivid and powerful incantations:

> Fierce Anthropophagi,
> Spectra, Diaboli,
> What scared St. Anthony,
> Hobgoblins, Lemures,
> Dreams of Antipodes,
> Night-riding Incubi
> Troubling the fantasy,
> All dire illusions
> Causing confusions;
> Figments heretical,
> Scruples fantastical,
> Doubts diabolical,
> Abaddon vexeth me,
> Mahu perplexeth me,
> Lucifer teareth me . . .

This ought to have the potency of a spell, even if only of a serio-comic one such as Hood or Gilbert might have brought off; Lamb fails to bring it off—most probably because his ear was a faulty instrument, though possibly because his heart was not in the writing of verse and his patience was exhausted by what he had spun out of himself long before it had been hammered into final shape. Very occasionally a line stands up from a poem with so striking an effect as to suggest that this time true poetry has for a moment been touched—

> Defiling with the world my virgin heart;[1]

and there are other moments when a sudden burst of metrical rhetoric partially deludes the critical sense:

> 　The man of parts,
> Poet, or prose declaimer, on his couch
> Lolling, like one indifferent, fabricates
> A heaven of gold, where he, and such as he,
> Their heads encompassed with crowns, their heels
> With fine wings garlanded, shall tread the stars
> Beneath their feet, heaven's pavement, far removed
> From damned spirits, and the torturing cries
> Of men, his breth'ren, fashioned of the earth,
> As he was, nourish'd with the self-same bread,
> Belike his kindred or companions once—
> Through everlasting ages now divorced,
> In chains and savage torments to repent
> Short years of folly on earth. There groans unheard
> In heav'n, the saint nor pity feels, nor care,
> For those thus sentenced—pity might disturb
> The delicate sense and most divine repose
> Of spirits angelical.[2]

---

[1] From the early *Innocence* sonnet.
[2] From *Composed at Midnight*.

Here is a distinct echo of Milton, but crude and diluted and confused with harsher sounds. Crudity of another sort is present in the polemics of *A Ballad: Noting the Difference of Rich and Poor, in the Ways of a Rich Noble's Palace and a Poor Workhouse*, which, as a piece of social criticism, is worthless since it sets up conventional puppets whereas it might have dealt directly with the problem of want and poverty. If its right to the designation *ballad* is admitted at all, it belongs to the nineteenth-century street peddler's stock-in-trade and not to the old English ballad tradition. Lamb rarely, if ever, proffered a reach-me-down moral system or a biased partisan view of society in his prose, but his tact was much more inclined to fail him when he turned to verse, and he was evidently one of those writers who are more amenable to literary discipline in prose than in verse. In view of his matchless familiarity with the Elizabethan and Jacobean dramatists it is a little surprising that his verse shows so few signs of influence from that direction. Only one among his poems could be regarded as deriving in some very slight degree from the sixteenth to seventeenth century lyrical manner:

SHE IS GOING

For their elder Sister's hair
Martha does a wreath prepare
Of bridal rose, ornate and gay:
Tomorrow is the wedding day:
  She is going.

Mary, youngest of the three,
Laughing idler, full of glee,
Arm in arm does fondly chain her,
Thinking, poor trifler, to detain her—
  But she's going.

L

Vex not, maidens, nor regret
Thus to part with Margaret.
Charms like your's can never stay
Long within doors: and one day
    You'll be going.

This appeared in *Album Verses* in 1830, and another lyric to the same (or another) unidentified Margaret was dated by Lamb from Edmonton in October 1834, within a few weeks of his death. It is the most delicate light poem he ever wrote, and is also, probably, the last of his verse compositions:

Margaret, in happy hour
Christen'd from that humble flower
    Which we a daisy call!
May thy pretty name-sake be
In all things a type of thee,
    And image thee in all.

Like *it* you show a modest face,
An unpretending native grace:—
    The tulip and the pink,
The china and the damask rose,
And every flaunting flower that blows,
    In the comparing shrink.

Of lowly fields you think no scorn;
Yet gayest gardens would adorn,
    And grace, wherever set,
Home-seated in your lonely bower,
Or wedded—a transplanted flower—
    I bless you Margaret!

The word "pretty", which has sunk into disrepute in our less-pleasantly simple generation, is one which can aptly be used not only of the Margaret lyric but also, in a more pathetic sense, of the lines (referring to Thomas Hood's first child) *On an Infant Dying as Soon as Born*. Lamb was not an impressive elegiast, nor would an elaborate memorial ode have been suitable to this occasion, but he did employ what can in the best sense be called a pretty fancy, and a delicately pathetic one also, in the thought here expressed of laying the child's unused toys and garments upon its coffin:

> Rites, which custom does impose,
> Silver bells and baby clothes;
> Coral redder than those lips,
> Which pale death did late eclipse;
> Music framed for infants' glee,
> Whistle never tuned for thee;
> Though thou want'st not, thou shalt have them,
> Loving hearts were they which gave them.
> Let not one be missing; nurse,
> See them laid upon the hearse
> Of infant slain by doom perverse.
> Why should kings and nobles have
> Pictured trophies to their grave;
> And we, churls, to thee deny
> Thy pretty toys with thee to lie,
> A more harmless vanity?

In this poem Lamb entirely succeeds in keeping a bright and flowerlike freshness for a fancy that might easily have become tinged by some hint of morbidity and decay. It does not surprise us to know—though it annoyed him a lot—that he incurred the charge of morbidity on account of another poem. This was *The Gipsy's Malison*, the most virile of all Lamb's verses. The sonnet (which is technically poor) scarcely needs the few words of explanatory introduction needed to point out that the poet here imagines a gipsy cursing (and forecasting a criminal's doom for) the child of a woman who has refused alms:

"Suck, baby, suck, mother's love grows by giving,
Drain the sweet founts that only thrive by wasting;
Black manhood comes when riotous guilty living
Hands thee the cup that shall be death in tasting.

Kiss, baby, kiss, mother's lips shine by kisses,
Choke the warm breath that else would fall in blessings;
Black manhood comes, when turbulent guilty blisses
Tend thee the kiss that poisons 'mid caressings.

Hang, baby, hang, mother's love loves such forces,
Strain the fond neck that bends still to thy clinging;
Black manhood comes, when violent lawless courses
Leave thee a spectacle in rude air swinging."

So sang a wither'd Beldam energetical,
And bann'd the ungiving door with lips prophetical.

This is a further instance of a potentially first-rate poem ruined by Lamb's maddening slackness about words and verse-forms. Apart from its slight nod in the direction of the Shakespearean sonnet pattern, *The Gipsy's Malison* can hardly be regarded as belonging to the category of sonnets. Indeed, it half suggests that Lamb either knew little or cared little about the requirements for a sonnet—except that it must be confined to fourteen lines and that it may, by Elizabethan license, consist of four quatrains and a rhyming couplet. If it had not limply pretended to be a sonnet and had limited itself to the first twelve lines, we should have been spared the feeble concluding lines with their hocking rhyme-words, and should be saved the necessity of protesting that the suggestion of a refrain in the three stanzas is inadmissible in a sonnet. As a twelve-line macabre lyric it would fall only little short of excellence in its kind, and its failure to hit the mark would be principally due, again, to Lamb's traitorous ear, which allowed "riotous guilty", "turbulent guilty" and "violent lawless" to pass without apprising him of (a) their ugly inharmony (which is not—what would have been most appropriate to the subject— deliberate discord) and (b) the absurdity of giving such stilted "literary" phrases to a violent cursing gipsy. An examination of Lamb's verse compositions provides very little evidence that he had grasped so much as an elementary notion of the nature of poetry from the poet's point of view. It is almost ununder-standable that he should have been thus disabled when we consider that his mature success as a prose-writer was due to the extraordinary cunning with which he matched matter and manner, with an emphasis (unguessed by many readers) upon *manner*. In prose he had a good deal to say and at the age of forty-five he found the way to say it. In verse he had something to say, but he never discovered how to say it. He would appear to have had a total in-comprehension of the way in which Poetry arises from its own discovery of the perfectly appropriate form in which to express itself. Apparently he went round looking for Poetry with one of Betty's candles, and he never found it because he never placed himself at the disposal of Poetry, nor invited it to find through him the channel it required. There need not be any doubt that Poetry wanted to produce a rhymed witch's curse and that it chose Lamb to be its agent for the purpose. It chose unwisely, however, for when Poetry whispered in Lamb's ear "Witch's curse", Lamb said "Certainly; we'll write a sonnet." Poetry objected, "I don't want to be a sonnet at present; I want to be a macabre poem in three quatrains." Lamb merely swept Poetry aside and muttered "Don't be silly. I said a sonnet; anything can be a sonnet at any time." So *The Gipsy's Malison* became, not really a sonnet, but a mistake.

Lamb might, with luck and more good sense in this matter, have become a very good verse-writer, but the high gods did not intend that he should be a poet.

§ 2

Little can or need be said concerning Charles Lamb's four plays. One, or perhaps two, might be resurrected as an act of piety for an anniversary celebration, but none could hope to hold the stage for more than a single performance and before a selected audience. All four are astonishingly naïve, and since Lamb's critical ability in regard to the stage cannot be denied, it must be supposed that the quality of his own plays is a reflection on the general standard of dramatic writing at the time. In fairness to his reputation, however, it must be stated that while three of his plays were considered for actual production, the only one that reached the boards seems, to a modern reader, by far the most unplayable. The *Pawnbroker's Daughter* might have done better, and *The Wife's Trial* better still.

John Woodvil, the first to be written (when he was about twenty-five) is labelled "*A Tragedy*";—one would like to know why. It is true that a death occurs in the piece, but although that event is the pivot upon which

the development turns, the death has no tragic pre-
liminaries or consequences, nor is it brought about
in a tragic fashion. Sir Walter Woodvil, a Devonshire
knight with Cromwellian sympathies, is outlawed at
the Restoration, and, disguised as a French lord, takes
refuge in Sherwood Forest; while his elder son John
enters (riotously) into possession of the family estate
and is instrumental in betraying his father to two spies
who pose as friends. When the two confront Sir Walter
in the forest he falls down and dies, on learning of his
son's apparent treachery. John, hearing this news,
repents and becomes a reformed character. Lamb
had obviously cribbed his situations—exiled lords in
forest and resolute maiden in male attire—from the
Elizabethans, but he had neither their skill in weaving
intrigue nor their lyrical fancy—nor, of course, their
seemingly natural ability in the handling of blank
verse. Not for a moment does *John Woodvil* become
anything better than a lifeless parody of Greene, or
a wooden travesty of Shakespeare. Here is John at the
end of a soliloquy (having apparently just recollected
a piece from *Hamlet*):

> Great spirits ask great play-room. Who could sit,
> With these prophetic swellings in my breast,
> That prick and goad me on, and never cease,
> To the fortunes something tells me I was born to?
> Who, with such monitors within to stir him,
> Would sit him down, with lazy arms across,
> A unit, a thing without a name in the state,
> A something to be govern'd, not to govern. . . .

No play with a famous signature ever ended more
weakly than Lamb allowed *John Woodvil* to do, in the
long-considered final version printed in 1818. John,

having been reconciled to Margaret, describes in the last words of the piece how he was brought to repentance by going to church very early on Sunday morning:

> So entering in, not without fear,
> I past into the family pew,
> And covering up my eyes for shame,
> And deep perception of unworthiness,
> Upon the little hassock knelt me down,
> Where I so oft had kneel'd,
> A docile infant by Sir Walter's side;
> And, thinking so, I wept a second flood
> More poignant than the first;
> But afterwards was greatly comforted.
> It seem'd, the guilt of blood was passing from me
> Even in the act and agony of tears,
> And all my sins forgiven.

CURTAIN.

It may be doubted whether any tragedy could be strong enough to cope with a "little hassock" and a "docile infant".

In one respect Lamb was a true descendant of the Elizabethans: word-play fascinated him. He gave vent to this in each of the other three dramatic pieces, though only passingly in *The Wife's Trial*. *Mr. H.* depends absolutely upon verbal humour, but so miserably thin a joke could only have been carried off by an O. Henry, who would have employed the devices of suspense and a snap-ending, or by a P. G. Wodehouse using all the resources of an audacious vocabulary. A presentable and apparently rich young man who refuses to be known by any other name than "Mr. H.", launches himself into society at Bath and becomes fashionable and much wooed. The whole place is agog to discover his full name. The only dramatic possibility in such an idea would be either (for farce) to keep the secret until the latest possible moment and then give it some absurd twist, or (for strong drama) to make the mysterious initial stand for some name with a well-known and horrifying significance that would freeze the marrow of those who had been hangers-on to the strange visitor. Lamb—poor Lamb, as we may say strictly for this instance only—could neither keep the secret long enough nor make anything of it when it was discovered. Mr. H. was Mr. Hogsflesh—a dislikeable name, but (especially as it was a well-known name in Lamb's day) not one to make H.'s acquaintances immediately turn their backs upon him in disgust. The farce arrives at a "happy ending" when Melesinda is reconciled to Hogsflesh, on news being brought that a royal warrant has been granted, authorising him to change his name to Bacon. The quality of the play and its wit may be judged by this passage—probably the most favourable that could be found:

MR. H.—Landlord, I must pack up tonight; you will see all my things got ready.

LANDLORD.—Hope your Honor does not intend to quit the Blue Boar—sorry anything has happened.

MR. H.—He has heard it all.

LANDLORD.—Your Honor has had some mortification, to be sure, as a man may say; you have brought your pigs to a fine market.

MR. H.—Pigs!

LANDLORD.—What then? take old Pry's advice, and never mind it. Don't scorch your crackling for 'em, Sir.

MR. H.—Scorch my crackling! A queer phrase; but I suppose he don't mean to affront me.

LANDLORD.—What is done can't be undone; you can't make a silken purse out of a sow's ear.

MR. H.—As you say, Landlord, thinking of a thing does but augment it.

LANDLORD.—Does but *hogment* it, indeed, Sir.

MR. H.—*Hogment* it! damn it, I said, augment it.

LANDLORD.—Lord, Sir, 'tis not every body has such gift of fine phrases as your Honor, that can lard his discourse.

MR. H.—Lard!

LANDLORD.—Suppose they do smoke you——

MR. H.—Smoke me?

LANDLORD.—One of my phrases; never mind my words, Sir, my meaning is good. We all mean the same thing, only you express yourself one way, and I another, that's all. The meaning's the same; it is all pork.

MR. H.—That's another of your phrases, I presume.
(*Bell rings and the Landlord is called for.*)

LANDLORD.—Anon, anon.

MR. H.—Oh, I wish I were anonymous.

For Lamb, *Mr. H.* must be regarded as a porcine misadventure, which did not, fortunately, deter him from returning to the subject of pig long afterwards in one of his best and most famous essays.

Mr. H. came on at Drury Lane in 1806; *The Pawnbroker's Daughter*, Lamb's next attempt at drama (again a farce) was published in *Blackwood's Magazine* in 1830. In addition to the pawnbroker's daughter (Marian Flint) who elopes, taking with her some of the unredeemed jewels pledged in her father's business, there is a Maria Flyn (something turns on the similarity of names), a comic humanitarian butcher, Cutlet, and

Miss Flyn's lover, Pendulous, who has by a miscarriage of justice been sent to the gallows and cut down when a last moment reprieve arrives. But Pendulous feels permanently disgraced by his experience, and Miss Flyn, to be level with him, and cure him of false delicacy, gets herself arrested in place of Marian for the supposed jewel theft. In the last police-court scene, after the confusion has been cleared up, Pendulous says:

> False delicacy adieu! The true sort, which this lady has manifested—by an expedient which at first sight might seem a little unpromising, has cured me of the other. We are now on even terms.
>
> Miss Flyn.—And may——
>
> Pendulous.—Marry,—I know it was your word.
>
> Miss Flyn.—And make a very quiet——
>
> Pendulous.—Exemplary——
>
> Miss Flyn.—Agreeing pair of——
>
> Pendulous.—Acquitted Felons.
>
> Flint.—And let the prejudiced against our profession acknowledge, that a money-lender may have the heart of a father; and that in the casket, whose loss grieved him so sorely, he valued nothing so dear as (*turning to Marian*) one poor domestic jewel.

Curtain.

Since *Mr. H.*, Lamb had realised that more substantial material was required for a play than he had there, and *The Pawnbroker's Daughter* is slightly less deficient in that respect. The play has body and there is a pattern in it, though Lamb had not learned that a farce must be played in its own key. Whereas *Mr. H.* has a bias toward straight comedy of a low grade, *The Pawnbroker's Daughter* strikes the note of romantic drama and is hardly more in the key of farce than *John Woodvil* is in the key of tragedy. The reasonable conclusion is that Lamb, as a writer, was far too much of a wandering disposition ever to become a dramatist. The infinite discursiveness of the Elia essays is their hall-mark and sign of perfection, but a dramatist must submit his material to close compression. A good play should be packed with stuff in orderly and precise arrangement, and it must be written and played in the key of high comedy, low comedy, romantic drama, farce, tragedy or whatever form the writer has chosen. A play cannot afford to skip about irresponsibly or to ignore its proper key; nor can it afford (except when written by a dramatist with a special genius for light dialogue) to foist itself upon the stage with threadbare material. *The Wife's Trial* is more satisfying (at least in reading) than the other plays by Lamb, because it has more substance—it is founded on Crabb's tale, *The Confidant*—and suspense is maintained until an advanced point in the story. From our modern viewpoint it is a preposterous piece, but within its own limits it succeeds fairly well. Mrs. Frampton, a widowed friend who comes to stay at the Wiltshire home of the Selbys, appears to have some secret hold upon young Mrs. Selby. In the hope of ridding the house of one who has become an aggressive nuisance, Mr. Selby, abetted by his sister, pretends to develop an affectionate interest in the widow and thus induces her to reveal the secret. She falsely declares that Mrs. Selby had committed bigamy by marrying Selby while a previous young husband was still alive, but Selby had in the meantime learned that his predecessor died abroad just before the second marriage. He uses an elaborate subterfuge in the last scene in order to expose Mrs.

Frampton's treachery; and the play ends with happiness and pardons all round. Neither here nor elsewhere in his dramatic pieces does Lamb succeed (one doubts if he so much as attempted) in creating a character that could be taken for a living creature. The characters have names and they are given words to say, but we feel under no compulsion to associate the words or names with the characters. In effect, Lamb sets up (to take the last play as example) four posts and to each post he affixes a label. *Post I*—Mr. Selby; *Post II*—Katherine, his wife; *Post III*—Lucy, his sister; *Post IV*—Mrs. Frampton, a widow. Then, by a ventriloquial pretence, words appear to come from the posts, but no one can believe that Post I *is* Mr. Selby, or that it is, at any moment, other than Post I.

The failures of great men have a special interest of their own, and Lamb's plays have such an interest. If, however, they are to be assessed alongside other men's successful plays, it is impossible to regard them as more than elementary essays in stage carpentry.

CHAPTER NINE

ROSAMUND GRAY—CHILDREN'S BOOKS —CRITICISM

§ I

WHEREAS the essays of Elia make an immediate effect upon the reader by some well-studied artifice in the first lines, Lamb's earlier works require some patience from the reader. Many who have opened *Rosamund Gray* with high expectations based upon a love of Elia must have felt, from the opening sentence, that this simple tale is a little absurd, rather dull, and somewhat clumsy—if not absurd, dull and clumsy without qualification. But second impressions are sounder than first in reference to these early works of Lamb, and a re-reading of *Rosamund Gray* shows that the magic which was afterwards to be Elia is not absent from this apprentice piece. Two or three things need to be remembered: *First,* that the tale cannot suitably be read without keeping in mind the type of popular fiction current at the end of the eighteenth century: a type, depending upon an unsubtle use of sensibility, which Jane Austen was to kill so exquisitely. "Sensibility", though not easily to be separated from sentimentality in the lesser novels of the period, was, in fact, different. Sensibility, if we care to put it thus, was sentimentality without the more maudlin element of sob-stuff so freely supplied by later novelists of the best-seller variety. Sentimentality, as nowadays disliked and mistrusted by the intellectuals, is a shameless exploitation of emotion in excess. The sensibility school of a century or so ago had some control behind their work. We might prefer that they should have had more, or a different kind of control—yet control there was. The kind of control, as can be seen from *Rosamund Gray*, which originated in an unsophisticated and unquestioning acceptance of the humane tenets of religion, with all that this implies in the way of a simplification of human nature. Good young people (to take the obvious example from *Rosamund Gray*) loved their grandmothers and behaved dutifully toward them; they were so modest and innocent that they fluttered dove-like under the dawning approach of love; they fell with the inertness of ripe peaches into the hands of their seducers; having been thus simply dishonoured they pined away and died; and their desolated legitimate lovers, instead of hunting down and slitting the throats of the ravishers, gave themselves to sad-eyed celibacy and good works and forgivingly attended the miserable death-beds of the villains. It was a convention—unacceptable to us, but no more absurd in relation to the facts of human behaviour than the more modern convention which causes fictional heroines to cast their virtue overboard at the first eagerly sought opportunity, instead of putting it into warm flannels and hugging it with large-eyed and timorous concern. All conventions in fiction are absurd, except to the generation that practises them; and, when approached from its proper angle, *Rosamund Gray* is most assuredly not more absurd than *The Sheik*; the difference is merely the difference between a generation which breakfasted contentedly on bread-and-milk and a generation which prefers (or prefers to think it prefers) devilled kidneys. *Rosamund Gray* is a positive tale with positive merits. What we think of it depends upon our angle of approach; and the angle of approach depends upon whether the modern reader is or is not familiar with the then current convention which had been popularised by Henry Mackenzie in *The Man of Feeling* and in the story referred to in *Rosamund Gray, Julie de Roubigné*. Amplifying the points already touched upon, the *second* thing to be remembered is that Lamb's brief story was written during a critical time in his own individual experience, and that his deep responses to that experience (the killing of his mother by the frenzied Mary) definitely coloured the fictional convention with the light of personal conviction. Lamb was then in a mood —in so far as it was not second nature for him—to believe and assert that the observance of family duty and domestic virtue was the proper and imperative lot of man. The *third* thing to be realised is that the literary convention of sensibility was coupled, and not only in Lamb, with an intense sincerity. It was not merely a convention adopted in order to ensure popularity and large sales; it did correspond to some deadly earnestness in both writers and readers.

If *Rosamund Gray* is approached along such lines, the present-day reader will not fall into the unprofitable error of judging it inappropriately from the standpoint of present-day notions. But there is more to say. *Rosamund Gray* is not by any means disposed of when defensive apologies have been made. It is necessary to repeat that it has positive merits; at moments there comes a flash of that pure engagingness which is peculiar to Lamb; and it has a quality which might be called a breadlike wholesomeness, but had better be called, more tritely, sweetness and light. This quality imposes itself upon the reader, even though something within him may cry out that it is dated and old-fashioned stuff. The following passage is from one of the letters used by Lamb to tell part of the story. The writer is Elinor, the sister of Allan Clare, Rosamund's excellent young lover:

. . . Continue to write to me, my sweet cousin. Many good thoughts, resolutions, and proper views of things, pass through the mind in the course of the day, but are lost for want of committing them to paper. Seize them, Maria, as they pass, these Birds of Paradise, that show themselves and are gone, . . . and make a grateful present of the precious fugitives to your friends.

To use a homely illustration, just rising in my fancy, . . . shall the good housewife take such pains in pickling and preserving her worthless fruits, her walnuts, her apricots, and quinces . . . and is there not much spiritual housewifery in treasuring up our mind's best fruits, . . . our heart's meditations in its most favoured moments?

This said simile is much in the fashion of the old Moralisers, such as I conceive honest Baxter to have been, such as Quarles and Withers were, with their curious, serio-comic, quaint emblems. But they sometimes reach the heart, when a more elegant simile rests in the fancy.

Not low and mean, like these, but beautifully familiarised to our conceptions, and condescending to human thoughts and notions, are all the discourses of our LORD . . . conveyed in parable, or similitude, what easy access do they win to the heart, through the medium of the delighted imagination! speaking of heavenly things in fable, or in simile, drawn from earth, from objects *common, accustomed.*

Life's business, with such delicious little interruptions as our correspondence affords, how pleasant it is! . . . why

M

can we not paint on the dull paper our whole feelings, exquisite as they rise up?

If matters of literary technique are to be discussed in this association, the obvious objection here is that the letter is not in the style of an Elinor Clare, but in that of Lamb himself; and this is a criticism to be made also of *Rosamund Gray* as a whole—that the author never hesitates to suspend the narrative for the purpose of interpolating his own meditations. What in another man's work would be a fault is, however, in this case, the best of merits. *Rosamund Gray* interests us because there is in it so much of Lamb himself, however undeveloped, and he was already endowed with somewhat of that extraordinary persuasiveness which was among the chief graces of Elia. To one who is not in the least inclined to commend an attitude of resignation, *Rosamund Gray* does nevertheless appear as a book which teaches most admirably a beautiful resignation; and it was precisely in a mood of beautiful resignation that Lamb wrote it. Half its effect, if not all, arises from our sense of its palpitating nearness to Lamb's deepest feelings at the most critical stage of his life. Written as it was within the fictional conventions of the late eighteenth-century, one of its inevitable ingredients is a dimly-seen figure of villainy, Matravis. He it is that encompasses the ruin of Rosamund. Has it ever been remarked that there is a slight resemblance in two respects between Lamb's tale and Hardy's *Tess of the D'Urbervilles*? Lamb's hero is Allan Clare; Hardy's Angel Clare. Tess is waylaid by the villain out-of-doors at night; so is Lamb's heroine. The episode in *Rosamund Gray* is thus described:

Matravis had, till now, been content to be a villain within the limits of the law—but, on the present occasion, hot fumes of wine, co-operating with his deep desire for revenge, and the insolence of an unhoped-for meeting, overcame his customary prudence, and Matravis rose, at once, to an audacity of glorious mischief.

Late at night he met her, a lonely, unprotected virgin— no friend at hand—no place of refuge.

Rosamund Gray, my soul is exceeding sorrowful for thee—I loath to tell the hateful circumstances of thy wrongs. Night and silence were the only witnesses of this young maid's disgrace—Matravis fled.

Rosamund, polluted and disgraced, wandered, an abandoned thing, about the fields and meadows till day-break. Not caring to return to the cottage, she sat herself down before the gate of Miss Clare's house in a stupor of grief.

The story of Tess's betrayal is told in a different temper, but in not altogether dissimilar terms:

Darkness and silence ruled everywhere around. Above them rose the primeval yews and oaks of The Chase, in which were poised gentle roosting birds in their last nap; and about them stole the hopping rabbits and hares. But, some might say, where was Tess's guardian angel? where was the Providence of her simple faith? Perhaps, like that other god of whom the ironical Tishbite spoke, he was talking, or he was pursuing, or he was in a journey, or peradventure he was sleeping and not to be awaked.

Why was it that upon this beautiful feminine tissue, sensitive as gossamer, and practically blank as snow as yet, there should have been traced such a coarse pattern as it was doomed to receive; why so often the coarse appropriates the finer thus, the wrong man the woman, the wrong woman the man, many thousand years of analytical philosophy have failed to explain to our sense of order.

It would be pleasant to believe that some old memory

of *Rosamund Gray* was lingering in Hardy's mind when he wrote *Tess*; but, even if that was not so, it would still be of interest and some value to compare these two treatments of the seduction theme, separated by a hundred years, and to consider, as a literary, philosophical and religious phenomenon, the totally changed attitude of mind which in the lapse of a century had been brought about.

§ 2

According to modern taste, *Rosamund Gray* might seem more in the nature of a moral tale for young people than a novel for grown-ups, but it was otherwise intended. Not until nearly ten years later did Charles Lamb begin to write for children, and when at length the *Tales from Shakespeare* were published, in 1807, his name on the title-page was less than half justified, for Mary was responsible for nearly three-quarters of the contents—Charles having made the versions of only *Lear*, *Macbeth*, *Timon of Athens*, *Romeo*, *Hamlet*, and *Othello*. In his own words he was also answerable for "occasionally a tail piece or a correction of grammar, for none of the cuts [illustrations] and all of the spelling". It has been assumed that the public attribution of credit to Charles alone was by her wish. Probably she was reluctant to forsake privacy in any way, since she was never publicly named during her lifetime as the author of her works (except for a few poems included with Charles's).

Tales from Shakespeare is a nearly successful attempt at an impossible task. Intended, not as a substitute for Shakespeare, but as an introduction to him, care was taken to use his own words wherever possible, and, when that was not feasible, to introduce only

such words as were in use in his day. It was impossible
to keep to this latter resolve in absolute strictness, but
when Charles had got into a fine narrative swing—
as in the *Hamlet* paraphrase—the influence of biblical
as well as Shakespearean English is evident. Except
for the mere purpose of recounting the main outlines
of the story in each of the plays subjected to treatment,
the scheme was certain to break down at some point;
and in regard to the Lambs' aims certain doubts must
arise. Whether they do provide "easy reading for very
young children" depends upon the individual child;
but the authors' method of spatchcocking pieces of
Shakespearean blank verse into passages of Lambian
prose would not be commendable on any pretext, and
it is deplorable that it should have been done "hoping
from its simple plainness to cheat the young readers
into the belief that they are reading prose". It is
inconceivable that the Lambs could really have meant
this, although there is other ground for suspecting
that Charles, at any rate, had no very sensitive ear
for blank verse. He was frosty about Marlowe, in
comparison with his enthusiasm for Beaumont and
Fletcher; and in the extracts from old plays in the
Dramatic Specimens he did not hesitate to leave out
single lines or groups of lines where he thought the
subject-matter permitted such excisions. That, however, is not the way of poetry; and it is difficult to
understand why the Lambs did not introduce occasional quoted passages of blank verse to stand as blank
verse instead of as disguised prose, thus enabling the
young ear to attune itself to poetry without the difficulty of reading long stretches of somewhat difficult
verse. The inadequacy (if no worse) of their method
of dealing with the great passages of poetry is pain-

fully apparent in a good many places, especially in Viola's lovely *Twelfth Night* speeches. Another serious shortcoming is the total disappearance of a number of characters whose absence could scarcely escape notice: Touchstone, Feste, Malvolio, Sir Toby Belch, Sir Andrew Aguecheek, Maria, Jacques, and others of like note—all indeed who are not in mid-stream of the main current of the story, however vital they may be to the play for other reasons. In dealing with *Hamlet*, Lamb had to omit nearly everything that is of psychological moment, and his doing so raises the question of whether, in fact, there is anything in Shakespeare which can be conveyed to "very young children", except a collection of stories. If this is so, then Lambs' do as well as any, emasculated though they are. A few things said in the preface are amusing to us who have departed from old-style family manners: "For young ladies, too, it has been my intention chiefly to write, because boys are generally permitted to use their father's libraries at a much earlier age than girls are." The author therefore begged assistance from young gentlemen in explaining difficult passages to the young ladies their sisters, and proposed that they should read actual scenes from the plays to supplement the tales—"carefully selecting what is proper for a young sister's ear".

Charles was also the collaborator with Mary in *Mrs. Leicester's School, or The History of Several Young Ladies, related by Themselves*, and, as before, his was the lesser part. The plan of the book is the old but excellent one of assembling a group of people and setting them to tell a succession of stories. In this case it is a group of young girls meeting at school for the first time and employing this means of getting to know one another.

Charles wrote three stories: *The Witch Aunt* (told by Maria Howe), *First Going to Church* (Susan Yates), *The Sea Voyage* (Arabella Hardy). *Mrs. Leicester's School* deserves more attention than it gets from present-day readers. If the book as a whole is too far from the modern manner to recapture a wide interest, then Lamb's three contributions should be extracted and made supplementary to Elia, with which they form an illuminating contrast, for they have much of the Elian quality without its ultimate magic. Some passages from *The Witch Aunt* have already been mentioned in the early biographical part of this present book, and Lamb recurred to the subject in the essay on *Witches, and other Night-Fears*. While realising that it is very often hard to keep on the track of Lamb in his hoverings between fiction and fact—especially when, as in *The Witch Aunt*, he transposes the sex of the principal character and speaks through the mouth of a girl—we know that much of this story is autobiographical, and part of the rest may be so. Lamb as a child certainly read the books he makes Maria Howe read; and this also may quite well be an actual recollection: "There was a book-closet which led into my mother's dressing-room. Here I was eternally fond of being shut up by myself, to take down whatever volumes I pleased, and pore upon them, no matter whether they were fit for my years or no, or whether I understood them." If this story does contain an authentic portrait of the young Lamb, he was, "a little unsociable, uncompanionable mortal". *First Going to Church*, which is set in the Lincolnshire fen district, is supposed to deal with his father's early days. The narrator conveys with great skill the child's impression of loneliness in the district and the sense of being cut-off from the active world by the great moor that stretched between the house and the nearest patch of civilisation. When from the distance comes the sound of St. Mary's bells, the infant thinks it is the songs of birds or angels from the air until she is told about churches. Then she longs to go to church, feeling herself deprived of something necessary to social rectitude; and her father having at length "ventured to set up a sort of carriage" they drive, one red-letter Sunday, to the great building which had once been a cathedral belonging to a monastery. And there, impressed by the statues of saints and bishops and the gargoyles outside, and by the memorials within, Susan Yates attends her first church service, sure that the attention of everyone present is rooted on herself. But though she concludes, in retrospect, that she was much too full of herself, she never afterwards felt a little outcast. Of the three stories, *The Witch Aunt* has most personal interest as belonging to Lamb's own childhood, but on other grounds it takes second place to *The Sea Voyage*, in which Arabella Hardy tells how she first came from the West Indies (her birthplace) when she was five. The young woman who was to accompany her fell ill just before the boat sailed, and as no other vessel was going to England that season Arabella, being the only passenger on board, goes in charge of the captain. On the passage across, the little girl was placed in the special care of one of the seamen, Charles Atkinson, whose gentle habits had caused him to be nicknamed Betsy by the other sailors. He tended Arabella with much tender devotion, and told her marvellous stories about sea monsters and fishes. She was fascinated by the changing colours of the sea, by the whales, by a lion and tiger caged aboard, and by the pet monkeys belonging to the crew. When she was terrified by rough weather Betsy told her that "the sea was God's bed and the ship our cradle", and the child was reassured. Not long before they reached England Betsy fell ill and died. He had told Arabella about his sweetheart Jenny, and poor Jenny, on receiving the sad news, went into a decline and also died. This sounds very bald in the telling, yet as Lamb tells it it is perfect. Unless for this occasion he received some sudden access of inventive ability and power of creative characterisation, it seems certain that he must have known the original of Betsy or had the germ of the story in vivid form from someone. Neither before nor afterward was Lamb to give so convincing a portrait of a human being in action—except in the case of George Dyer, and there, of course, he had the original frequently in his company.

Before he and Mary published (through Mrs. Godwin's firm) *Mrs. Leicester's School*, Charles had issued his prose version of part of Homer's *Odyssey*, *The Adventures of Ulysses*. Achieving nothing like the world-wide celebrity of the *Tales from Shakespeare*, the *Ulysses* has nevertheless kept its place among the introductions to Homer for juveniles. There were actually a much larger number of difficulties to overcome in the later task, but Lamb got over them by ignoring them. He knew no Greek, or next to none, so he was forced to leave Homer out of account entirely. He turned to Chapman's translation, and, from that, prepared a prose rendering of the best-known stories. Because there are no poetic sensibilities to be outraged (since the book after all does not pretend to be an introduction to Chapman) only one question arises in connection with *The Adventures of Ulysses*: does it tell the stories well? It does. Any boy (or grown-up, for that matter) who can read, without a quickening of the pulse, Lamb's account of Ulysses and his companions in the cave of Polyphemus must be in a sorry state.

The last of this sequence of juvenile books was *Poetry for Children* ("by the author of *Mrs. Leicester's School*"). Mary, once more, appears to have done the lion's share of the work, though only in one or two instances is the actual author of any particular poem known—either because Lamb acknowledged it as his in a letter, or because it was included in his *Collected Works* in 1818. In addition to the three certainties, Mr. Lucas attributes (with full reservations) about a score of the pieces to Charles. Perhaps the only general remark that need be made here, is to say that the volume compares most favourably with the very few good books of children's verse, and that in its own period only Jane and Ann Taylor's poems are in as high a class. The Lambs' verses for children are moral, but not insistently or priggishly so—and what is more rare, they sometimes rise near to the level of poetry. There is a deliciously fragrant beginning (probably by Mary),

> This rose-tree is not made to bear
> The violet blue, nor lily fair,
> Nor the sweet mignionette: . . .

and the piece called *Feigned Courage* (which is perhaps by Charles) has a most admirable concluding couplet. After describing how a certain small person who was boasting that he would be the image of the great heroes of legend and history, slightly hurt himself and subsided in tears, the poem ends

> Achilles weeps, great Hector hangs the head
> And the Black Prince goes whimpering to bed.

One of the merits of Lamb's *Poetry for Children* is that it does not appear to have one eye on a grown-up audience. There is not much in it to please the hundred-years-ago adult, because there is no deliberate moral hammering; and not much to please the present-day adult, because there are no playful tricks of rhythm, no "little language" and no condescending quaintness. If the book were to be read aloud to children nowadays the young auditors might be bored, though quite as likely they would not be, but the parental reader would at least be pleasantly conscious that he was not playing the moral confidence-trick upon immature minds nor outraging his own taste and intelligence.

§ 3

Introducing the *Specimens of English Dramatic Poets who Lived about the Time of Shakespeare*, Lamb observed: "I have expunged without ceremony all that which the writer had better never have written." That is to say he exercised a nineteenth-century moral censorship over the Elizabethans and their successors, although he was to be, some years later, the one who put up the most specious defence of the cuckoldry in which the Restoration dramatists dealt wholesale. The selected passages in the *Specimens* were accompanied by notes and comments, and these Lamb subsequently gathered together and reprinted in his *Works* under the heading *Characters of Dramatic Writers Con-*

temporary with Shakespeare. That title is more nearly accurate as a description of his aim than the earlier one had been, for it was not in fact with dramatic *poets* that he was most concerned but with *dramatic writers*—with drama more than with poetry. Lamb was usually disposed to get as confused when thinking about poetry as he was about art, and when he uses the word "poetry" in his criticism it cannot be accepted as prima facie evidence that he really means *poetry* as purists would mean it. In reference to the *Specimens* he says: "My leading design was, to illustrate what may be called the moral sense of our ancestors. To show in what manner they felt, when they placed themselves by the power of imagination in trying circumstances, in the conflicts of duty and passion, or the strife of contending duties; what sort of loves and enmities theirs were; how their griefs were tempered, and their full-swoln joys abated: how much of Shakespeare shines in the great men his contemporaries, and how far in his divine mind and manners he surpassed them and all mankind." This is all very well, all very laudable; there is no doubt every reason why Lamb should be commended for his design of showing the moral sense of our ancestors—but this has nothing or next to nothing to do with their poetry. It is only worth while pointing this out because he wrote, a few lines higher up in the preface, that he was anxious to give scenes (of passion, "interesting situations, serious descriptions") "more nearly allied to poetry than to wit". He proceeded to say that he also sought to rehabilitate such dramatists as Fletcher and Massinger and to demonstrate that they had been neglected while "old Marlowe" and others had been much cried up. We do not in any way underrate his achievement (the value of which as an essay in rediscovery it would be almost impossible to over-estimate) by suggesting that Lamb was not always perceptive enough as between the first-rate and the second-rate —a deficiency easily accounted for if his ear was truly defective in the presence of poetry. There is nothing in his notes to suggest that he recognised the poetic supremacy of Marlowe among Shakespeare's contemporaries. He discusses a number of matters in connection with Marlowe—the extravagance of passion, the pity and terror to which *Edward II* can move us, the treatment of Jews, atheism, the propriety of representing vicious characters—but he says nothing of the single quality in Marlowe which puts him above any Elizabethan stage-thunderer, his astonishing power as a manipulator of words, his faculty for turning blood and lust into the magnificences of poetry. On the evidence of the notes to the *Specimens* it would be a misapplication of terms to speak of Lamb as a critic at all, though he is undoubtedly an extremely interesting commentator: as on Marlowe's Barabbas—"It is curious to see a superstition wearing out. The idea of a Jew, which our pious ancestors contemplated with so much horror, has nothing in it now revolting. We have tamed the claws of the beast, and pared its nails, and now we take it to our arms, fondle it, write plays to flatter it; it is visited by princes, affects a taste, patronises the arts, and is the only liberal and gentle thing in Christendom." That is a nice piece of irony, but it is not literary criticism. It is with Lamb's comments on the drama as it is with his essays on pictures: there is a displayed interest in the *matter* but very little indeed in the *manner*, though without taking account of both there can be no perception of *the totality which is poetry*. At moments Lamb seems to approach the centre, as in this (of George Chapman): "He could not go out of himself, as Shakespeare could shift at pleasure, to inform and animate other existences, but in himself he had an eye to perceive and a soul to embrace all forms and modes of being"; but the moment passes. The well-known argument by Lamb that Shakespeare cannot with any real satisfaction be acted might with more validity have arisen from a conviction that poetry cannot be staged, but actually it only means that Lamb's imagination, like that of a good many other people, was active enough to perform Shakespeare's plays on the inner stage of his own consciousness, and that, therefore, he disliked by comparison any other person's outward interpretation. He apparently omits to notice that his argument, if it were sound, would turn chiefly against Shakespeare, not against the actors. Shakespeare wrote the plays primarily—in the first place, exclusively—for the stage. If they are unsuitable for the stage—or less suitable for that than for the printed book—then Shakespeare badly bungled his job. Though Lamb would scarcely have wished to maintain any such assertion, it is, nevertheless, the logical extension from his own argument. When in the essay *On the Tragedies of Shakespeare* he quotes a sonnet—

> Oh for my sake do you with Fortune chide,
> The guilty goddess of my harmful deeds
> That did not better for my life provide
> That public means which public manners breeds . . .

he does not, again, think of it as poetry, he thinks of it as an instance of "jealous self-watchfulness in our sweet Shakespeare"; and when Lamb, in another essay, writes on the poems of George Wither the attitude is similar, though he does there make some mention of the use of a particular measure for the clothing of what Wither had to say. But it is more especially in Lamb's review of Keats' *Lamia* volume that the true poverty of his equipment for the criticism of poetry is displayed. Beyond giving an account of the story in *Isabella* and making some quotations from that and *The Eve of Saint Agnes* and a few passing references to other poems, there is nothing. We look in vain for any inkling of recognition of Keats' true greatness as a poet—that is, of his power, shared with every other great poet, to create, by words of sense, other states of being beyond the world of sense.

CHAPTER TEN

THE WORKS OF CHARLES LAMB—
UNCOLLECTED ESSAYS

§ 1

THE two small octavo volumes—*The Works of Charles Lamb*—published by C. & J. Ollier in 1818 were made up in the following way:

VOLUME I

Poems (including some by Mary Lamb)
John Woodvil
Rosamund Gray
Recollections of Christ's Hospital

VOLUME II

Essays:

> *On the Tragedies of Shakespeare, Considered with Reference to their Fitness for Stage Representation*
>
> *Characters of Dramatic Writers Contemporary with Shakespeare*
>
> *Specimens from the Writings of Fuller, the Church Historian*
>
> *On the Genius and Character of Hogarth; with some Remarks on a Passage in the Writings of the Late Mr. Barry*
>
> *On the Poetical Works of George Wither*

Letters under assumed signatures:

The Londoner
On Burial Societies; and the Character of an Undertaker
On the Danger of Confounding Moral with Personal Deformity, with a hint to those who have the Framing of Advertisements for Apprehending Offenders
On the Inconveniences Resulting from Being Hanged
On the Melancholy of Tailors
Hospita on the Immoderate Indulgence of the Pleasures of the Palate
Edax on Appetite
Mr. H.

Comment has already been made in preceding chapters on the contents of the first volume and part of the second. Lamb's gatherings from Fuller are in line with his lifelong interest in the works of the seventeenth-century prose-writers who, in point of fact, came closer to his own temperament and interests than the dramatists whom he was also to plunder for the good of posterity without, however, capturing for himself anything of their poetic fire. We can quite well understand how delighted Lamb must have been to find in Fuller such sentences as that a negro is "the image of God cut in ebony"; that a certain divine "would pronounce the word *Damn* with such an emphasis as left a doleful echo in his auditors' ears a good while after"; and, of memory, "Philosophers place it in the rear of the head, and it seems the mine of memory lies there, because there men naturally dig for it, scratching it when they are at a loss". These and the numerous other aphorisms and paragraphs in this little anthology from Fuller give some reason for regret that Lamb did not compile a comprehensive

N

collection of passages from the prose-writers contemporary with Sir Thomas Browne.

The letter headed *The Londoner* and addressed to the Editor of *The Reflector* (written in 1802) was not published in the paper named, but in the *Morning Post* during the early days of Lamb's experiments in journalism. Like the rest of the *Letters under assumed Signatures* this piece is composed of such subject-matter as was afterwards to make the Elia essays, but, as already noted in connection with other early writings of Lamb, the true manner is absent—there is an indigested rawness which might pass for maturity in the works of some other author, but cannot be so regarded in comparison with Lamb's developed style of twenty years later. Yet it is after all a graceless business to complain that these productions of his young manhood are not perfect according to the Elia standard, when there is so much in them that is good. Already there was the characteristic habit of intermingling fact and fiction which was to make Elia at once a delight and a puzzlement. Writing as "A Londoner" in the letter under notice, Lamb alleged that he was born on Lord Mayor Show day, a fancy which enabled him to describe himself as "in some sort a speculative Lord Mayor of London: for though circumstances unhappily preclude me from the hope of ever arriving at the dignity of a gold chain and Spital Sermon, yet thus much will I say of myself in truth, that Whittington with his Cat (just emblem of vigilance and a furred gown) never went beyond me in affection which I bear to the citizens". Lamb was only twenty-seven when he wrote this, yet it was not too early for him to register his confirmed and inalienable love of the metropolis, to the derogation of rural places. There is one attractive autobiographical touch where he notes that his aversion to the country-side was only suspended for a while some years earlier when, as he says, "I had set my affections upon a charming young woman". From this temporary association between love and country affections he extracts the satisfaction of believing that it enabled him to understand what the poets mean when they praise nature in ecstatic terms. Lamb hastens to add that this contagion of rural passion no longer held him entranced. "I have no hesitation in declaring, that a mob of happy faces crowding up at the pit door of Drury-lane Theatre, just at the hour of six, gives me ten thousand sincerer pleasures, than I could ever receive from all the flocks of silly sheep that ever whitened the plains of Arcadia or Epsom Downs." It was a part of Lamb's special endowment that he could turn his limitations and deficiencies into admirable virtues, and while we might wish that his perceptions had been sharper than they were in regard to inanimate nature, few would be willing to sacrifice those praises of London which might have been lost if he had been a man of divided loyalties. But for the incontrovertible evidence of his friends, there would be ground for suspecting that Lamb's indifference to country scenes was a pose, seeing that no man ever held Izaak Walton in more affectionate esteem than Lamb did. Is it possible to love *The Compleat Angler* without also loving rural solitudes?

Though Lamb captured much from the seventeenth-century writers, he left much more uncaptured. Several of the *Letters* reprinted in the 1818 *Works* obviously came from a mind teeming with images drawn from Burton, Browne, and the rest, but in place of their grave meditations upon the majesty of death there is hardly more than a juvenile wit applied to gruesome morbidities. The seventeenth-century performed the miracle of being morbid without ceasing to be majestic, and what is a divine rhapsody in them degenerates sometimes to a graveyard grin in the early Lamb. On the whole it is singularly inappropriate to describe Lamb as a seventeenth-century man born out of his proper time. In some respects he was pure nineteenth-century, for neither in the sixteen hundreds nor seventeen hundreds—and certainly not in any previous age—could such an essay as that on *Burial Societies* have been written, and this not only because burial societies were of more recent origin. When, in this essay, Lamb quotes Sir Thomas Browne's "Man is a noble animal, splendid in ashes, and pompous in the grave", the sentence is apposite, but how different is the accent from anything in Lamb's own paragraphs surrounding the quotation. Browne could not have made a joke about death or the trappings of death, or if he had done so it could have been only such a joke as might pass without censure among the hierarchies of Eternity. Lamb, however, follows at once with a light disquisition upon coffin nails and such. And why not indeed?—when Lamb lightens these morbidities with so attractive an air. If he is not another Thomas Browne nor another Richard Burton nor another Donne, he is himself; he is not the trumpeter of death but its unabashed jester, with somewhat of that bitter-sweet melancholy that makes Shakespeare's clowns wise men as well as fools. And, like them, Lamb can flaunt a punning remark in the face of death itself. Of a few of Lamb's pet jokes we cannot but grow a little tired by the time we have traversed the whole of his writings. The central notion used in the essay *On the Inconvenience of Being Hanged* is the same as he used again in *The Pawnbroker's Daughter*: and is not a particularly good idea nor a particularly amusing joke, though it might be possible to claim that Lamb had some satirical and reformatory intention in writing this skit on certain side-issues of capital punishment. Rather more amusing are the letters attributed to Hospita and Edax, with their sly hits at vegetarianism and at parental overniceness in the bringing-up of children. Hospita, dismayed by the insatiable appetite of Edax, has carefully safeguarded her offspring from any contact with animal food: "a beef-steak is an absurdity to them; a mutton-chop, a solecism in terms; a cutlet, a word absolutely without any meaning"; nevertheless the eldest girl of ten is to be gently apprised of the debased appetites of mankind at large, and her mother is "in good hopes, when the proper season for her debut arrives, she may be brought to endure the sight of a roasted chicken or a dish of sweetbreads, for the first time, without fainting". This is just the sort of absurdity that Lamb with his contempt for humbug would pillory with gusto. Edax's own lament over his inordinate appetite seems to be almost wholly an invention, though there are a few passages which may embody in changed shape a memory of those many days when aunt Hetty trotted from the Temple to Newgate to bring her favourite nephew some tit-bit from the family table to augment the sparse fare at Christ's Hospital. Edax, recounting how the enormities of his appetite made him an object of derisive amazement among his friends, says, "My school-days come again, and the horror I used to feel when in some silent corner retired from the notice of

my unfeeling playfellows, I have sat to mumble the
solitary slice of gingerbread allotted to me by the
bounty of considerate friends, and have ached at heart
because I could not spare a portion of it, as I saw other
boys do to some favourite boy;—or if I know my own
heart, I was never selfish; never possessed a luxury
which I did not hasten to communicate to others;
but my food, alas! was none; it was an indispensable
necessary; I could have soon as spared the blood in my
veins, as have parted with that with my companions."
We have no evidence that the grown-up Lamb was a
remarkable trencherman, but he was far from insensible
to the pleasures of the palate. Food was not to him
so inexhaustible a subject as it was to Pepys, nor one
which afforded him so much exquisite pleasure, yet,
in more than the punning sense, it is impossible to think
of Lamb absolutely divorced from the table.

§ 2

Either because he became a more exacting self-
critic as time went on, or because he at length despaired
of successfully seeking the suffrages of the public, Lamb
left unpublished a number of pieces (contributed to
periodicals) which well bear comparison with some
of the essays discussed above. The lasting effect of
the failure of *Mr. H.* on Lamb's mind and spirits
has been noted, and one of his most deeply-felt autobiographical chapters is found in his contribution
to *The Reflector* (1811) entitled *On the Custom of Hissing
at the Theatres, with some Account of a Club of Damned
Authors*. This was written some five years after the
untimely eclipse of *Mr. H.*, but the recollection had not
been dimmed or made more pleasant during the

interval. Beneath the characteristic playful humour with which Lamb refers to the incident, there is a note of sharp protest, and he takes occasion to hit back at the public for what he describes as their outrageous way of expressing displeasure. Lamb says in effect that they ordered these things much better in Rome when they turned down their thumbs in disapprobation instead of, as the English do, degrading the expressive human voice "into a rival of the noises of silly geese, and irrational venomous snakes". Proceeding to particularise the rules framed by the Club of Damned Authors he sets down, as one of the chief tenets of that body: "That the public, or mob, in all ages, have been a set of blind, deaf, obstinate, senseless illiterate savages. That no man of genius in his senses would be ambitious of pleasing such a capricious, ungrateful rabble." Seldom does Lamb lay about him in so vigorous a manner, and that this was not merely mock fury we know from the similarly-phrased opinions now and again dropped into his letters. In general he preferred such methods as those adopted in *The Good Clerk, a Character* (also printed in *The Reflector* in 1811) where he commends as marks of virtue for the clerical office most of those qualities and observances which he himself signally failed to bring into operation during the years spent at East India House. Knowing as we do that Lamb was not inordinately punctual, we may judge with what half-acid satisfaction he remarked that a good clerk "riseth early in the morning . . . chiefly to the intent that he may be first at the desk. There is his post, there he delighteth to be unless when his meals, or necessity calleth him away; which time he alway esteemeth as lost, and maketh as short as possible. . . . His first ambition (as appeareth all along) is to be a good Clerk, his next a good Christian, a good Patriot, etc." This recipe, it may also be noted, prefaced a series of remarks upon Defoe's *The Complete English Tradesman*, which Lamb suggested is to be taken in an ironical sense and as a piece of covered satire—a plain hint for the reading of his own characterisation of the ideal clerkly person.

The mystifications set on foot by Lamb's habit of compounding fact and invention led in one case to a serious misunderstanding of his own character. This was in the well-known *Confessions of a Drunkard*, first printed in a quarterly publication *The Philanthropist* in 1813, reprinted by a teetotal enthusiast three years later, revived (while Lamb was in Paris) in the *London Magazine* in 1822 and included in a posthumous second edition of the *Last Essays of Elia* in 1835. It is a puzzling piece of writing, for it bears the mark of an almost passionate personal conviction and there are some things in it which beyond question relate to Lamb himself; equally there are sentences which we cannot but regard as either completely fictional or heavily exaggerated. "Behold me," he says, "in the robust period of life, reduced to imbecility and decay." There are two or three ways in which the dark portrait might be accounted for, without accepting it as a photographic representation of himself. It may have been written during one of Mary's illnesses, when Lamb was usually inclined to see the world and especially himself in the gloomiest colours; or he may have been labouring in one of those fits of self-induced disgust, when his inability to break away from drink and tobacco inclined him to condemn himself beyond cause or reason; or *The Confessions of a Drunkard* may have been written with what can be called a Salvation-Army motive, which causes well-intentioned people to slander and libel themselves so that they may become awful and forbidding examples to those whom they desire to safeguard from following similar sinful ways. Whatever the motive, or however near to or far from autobiographical exactitude, this essay is still one of the most forcible temperance tracts ever written, though neither by subject nor temper does it belong to the Elia period.

Also during Lamb's absence in France in the autumn of 1822, the Editor of the *London Magazine* reprinted *A Bachelor's Complaint of the Behaviour of Married People*, which belongs to a much earlier period and was omitted by Lamb from the 1818 collection. As this has commonly been accepted erroneously as being of the Elia period, comment upon it can be delayed until the next chapter, with the purpose of suggesting the noteworthy differences in style which separate the essays of 1821–5 from those of 1811 and thereabout. When Lamb gathered his essays for the first Elia volume he omitted a few of the new contributions made to the *London Magazine* and among these is one called *The Confessions of H. F. V. H. Delamore Esq.* written in the guise of a letter addressed by that gentleman to the editor and dated from Sackville Street, March 25, 1821. It is very brief, but bears the signature of Elia in every sentence, though it was not recognised as his until Bertram Dobell recovered it in 1903.[1] In the previous month's number of the *London Magazine* Elia's *Chapter on Ears* had appeared, and Delamore professes to be moved to proffer his confessions to the editor because of Elia's references

[1] See *Sidelights on Charles Lamb*, by Bertram Dobell.

to the pillory. In terms of a fantastically overstressed sense of having disgraced his ancestral name, Henry Francis Vere Harrington Delamore places it on record that

Once——
these legs with Kent in the play, though for far less ennobling considerations, did wear "cruel garters".

Yet I protest it was but for a thing of nought—a fault of youth, and warmer blood—a calendary inadvertance I may call it—or rather a temporary obliviousness of the day of the week—timing my Saturnalia amiss——

Streets of Barnet, infamous for civil broils, ye saw my shame!—did not your Red Rose rise again to dye my burning cheek?

It was but for a pair of minutes, or so—yet I feel, I feel, that the gentry of the Delamores is extinguished for ever?——

Try to forget it, reader.——

The special interest in this is that there is reason for believing that once, on a Sunday morning, when Lamb walked out to Barnet with one of his fellow-clerks, they indulged in some high-spirited exploit which earned Lamb the brief punishment Delamore so affectingly laments. This, of course, lends an amusing ironical colour to Lamb's assertion in the *Chapter on Ears*, "I was never, I thank my stars, in the pillory". He was, however, it appears, on the stated occasion, in the stocks. He returned to this topic of public punishment in the *London Magazine* in 1825 in a contribution entitled *Reflections in the Pillory*—an Elia essay not reprinted by Lamb. It contains this passage: "O Pillory, 'tis thee I sing! Thou younger brother to the gallows, without his rough and Esau palms; that with ineffable contempt surveyest beneath thee the

grovelling stocks which claims presumptuously to be
of thy great race. Let that low wood know, that thou
are far higher born! Let that domicile for groundling
rogues and base earth-kissing varlets envy thy prefer-
ment, not seldom fated to be the wanton baiting-
house, the temporary retreat, of poet and of patriot."
Recalling his Barnet misadventure in the privacy of
his own mind, Lamb no doubt derived a good deal of
half-secret amusement from his depreciation of "the
grovelling stocks", which represented his own nearest
approach to the high dignity of the pillory in which
Defoe and other distinguished predecessors of Lamb
had stood.

Signed "Suspensurus", there appeared in the *London
Magazine* in April 1825 a very short piece headed
The Last Peach, in which the writer, who purports to
be a bank clerk, represents himself as troubled lest he
should be tempted to commit some defalcation that
will bring him to the gallows—not because he has any
need or lust for money but because he is haunted by
the memory of an incident in his early childhood.
"Suspensurus" was Charles Lamb, and the location
of the episode so delightfully described in *The Last
Peach* was Blakesware in Hertfordshire: "When a
child I was once let loose, by favour of a Nobleman's
gardener, into his Lordship's magnificent fruit garden,
with free leave to pull the currants and the goose-
berries; only I was interdicted from touching the
wall fruit. Indeed, at that season (it was the end
of Autumn) there was little left. Onlyon the South
wall (can I forget the hot feel of the brickwork?)
lingered the one last peach. Now peaches are a fruit
I always had, and still have, an almost utter aversion
to. There is something to my palate singularly harsh

and repulsive in the flavour of them. I know not by what demon of contradiction inspired, but I was haunted by an irresistible desire to pluck it. Tear myself as often as I would from the spot, I found myself still recurring to it, till, maddening with desire (desire I cannot call it) with wilfulness rather—without appetite—against appetite, I may call it—in an evil hour I reached out my hand, and plucked it. Some few raindrops just then fell; the sky (from a bright day) became overcast; and I was a type of our first parents after the eating of that fatal fruit. I felt myself naked and ashamed; stripped of my virtue, spiritless. The downy fruit, whose sight rather than savour had tempted me, dropt from my hand, never to be tasted. All the commentators in the world cannot persuade me but that the Hebrew word in the second chapter of Genesis, translated apple, should be rendered peach."

Among the other miscellaneous pieces which have been gathered into book form only since Lamb's death, perhaps the most interesting is the series of papers signed Lepus, contributed to *The New Times* in 1825 and salvaged some three-quarters of a century later by Mr. E. V. Lucas for his complete edition of Lamb's writings. The first of this group is *Many Friends* —one of Lamb's several good-humored plaints on the matter of his superfluity of visitors. This was followed by *Readers Against the Grain*, containing reflections upon the growth of bookshops in the metropolis where cheap reprints of the English novelists, poets and historians were then being made available for those of small means. Lamb felt that while the consequent extension of the reading public might be beneficial in some respect, it had its other side. Reading was in danger of becoming not merely a habit but a fashion, the thing to do, leading to the publication of a "never ending flow of thin novelties", and to the growth of a custom of reading merely that the readers might say they had read. Lamb preferred the old days of his own youth when, at some expense and difficulty, people "read because they liked reading". He would rather have it that young men should continue to be, as they were then, playgoers, punch-drinkers, cricketers and so forth, than that they should be "readers against the grain, who yet *must* read or be thought nothing of—who, crawling through a book with tortoise pace go creeping to the next Review to learn what they shall say of it".

CHAPTER ELEVEN

ELIA

§ 1

NEXT to Dickens, Elia is of all English prose-writers probably the one to whom the average reader takes most kindly without authoritative prompting. It would be useless to seek the reason for this exclusively in either the personal qualities of Lamb himself or in his choice of subject-matter—important though both these factors are. Lamb's virtues and failings would not supply literary material magically attractive in itself, and his chosen topics might more easily be dull than engaging. And, anyhow, he had been writing about not unsimilar topics for many years before substantial success came to him. Why should it have come in 1821 and not before? The suggestion has already been made that he had not till then reached the point at which memory could be made to yield the mature fruits of contemplation. But memory was far from doing all; it required the aid of literary craft. Much used to be said, and still is said, concerning Lamb's allusiveness; his habit of echoing, and quoting with a difference, the old writers. The charm of this is not to be gainsaid, yet of every hundred who read him with enjoyment it is doubtful if more than ten catch the echo, or have knowledge enough to observe more than a few of the allusions. If this were all, it would be as likely to impose a bar to Lamb's popularity as to assist it. A comparison between his earlier style and his later shows immediately an interesting difference; and the difference consists largely in his much-increased use of parenthesis. The technical secret of Elia may indeed be said to lie in the discovery of how effective a parenthetical style can be when suitably employed; and it is somewhat of a paradox to realise that although Lamb is accounted one of the greatest of English prose-writers, his prose, when strictly considered according to accepted academic standards, is bad prose. That is to say it would be bad prose if written by anyone but Lamb. This reflection raises again in an acute form the whole problem of prose style. It is useless to attempt to discover a single formula for the guidance of literary aspirants which will cover the prose of Defoe, Swift, Addison, Pater, and others who are accepted as good stylists. In the end we have to take refuge in the classic but rather unhelpful admission that the style is the man. A writer can only use with recognisable fitness the particular literary style which is accordant with his personality, mood and intention: the homespun of Swift and Defoe, perfect for themselves, would be ludicrously inadequate and inappropriate for a Sir Thomas Browne. There is no final definition of "good" prose style, except to say that a good prose writer is one who has discovered his own right style. Appropriateness is all. Perhaps it is not out of place to remember in connection with the Elia essays that, as a conversationalist, Lamb was troubled with a stammer, and it was therefore physically impossible for him to pour out a stream of smooth-flowing and uninterrupted sentences. The characteristic style of Elia is the translation of that stammer into literature. As Elia, Lamb at once veiled himself and discovered himself. By using another's name he was able to reveal himself freely without the distasteful handicap of consciously exhibiting himself; while at the same time he discovered that his only freedom as a writer lay in inventing a method whereby he could talk on paper in a manner corresponding with that which his physical impediment had made natural to him in speech. His previous failures—or, at best, only partial successes—had been very largely due to his attempt to write as other men wrote. But this was a useless undertaking for one so intensely personal as Lamb in his approach to life and literature. He needed to write, not as other men wrote, but as Charles Lamb himself was accustomed to talk. And those parentheses which run their intermittent horizontals through the pages of Elia give us, exactly, the sense that Lamb is not writing for us but talking to us. He is the Ancient Scrivener to whom the reader, held by a dreaming eye, listens like a three-years' child while the Scrivener hath his will. As Elia, Lamb the man of sentiment discovered a method by which he could appear to translate his sentiment into the accents of familiar talk; the utmost skill is behind it, comprised in that apparent superfluity of parenthetical dashes. The result is that these essays have, for the most part, the suggestion of a continuous impromptu, not something deliberately considered by a literary person and set down with deliberate literary intent. If this is prose with a stammer, however, it is not prose struggling against a handicap. For the first time in his life, Lamb became capable of achieving some of the true effects of poetry. *Elia* is not plain prose nor can it be rendered into plain prose, any more than true poetry can be paraphrased into prose of any sort. Elian prose at its best is a new creation. While, for the greater part of its length, we have on the plane of everyday meaning a precise idea of what Elia is saying, he is also frequently suggesting far more than he says. Some of his sentences are just as incapable of logical analysis as poetry is. What he says becomes relatively unimportant in comparison with the emotional overtones carried by the sentences. What, for example, is the "use", descriptively, in relation to the South Sea House, of such sentences as these: "Peace to the manes of the BUBBLE! Silence and destitution are upon thy walls, proud house, for a memorial!" Yet if it *tells* nothing about the South Sea House it nevertheless *conveys* all. This is something not intellectualised, not seeking the interpretative functions of logic or reason, but something heard in the heart and felt along the blood. Prose, plain prose, asks the attention of the mind and little but the mind; plain prose, it is agreed, has no right to make any appeal outside the mind. But the prose of Elia is continuously appealing to other faculties. We have suggested that it is bad prose. Of course it is; one could not write a business letter thus. But one could write a psalm or a prophecy. In a well-known passage, Ruskin once enjoined upon young people the imperative necessity of probing into the meaning of every word they read, though Ruskin is himself one of the last writers upon whom such a particularity could be tested with encouraging results. Ruskin's injunction was of course an absurd one, and its absurdity would be evident if applied to a single page of *Elia*. The mean-

o

ing of Elia may be present in the words, but that something beyond meaning which we can only all too loosely call "significance" is not in the words; it is, what?—an aura surrounding them?—an aroma rising from them?—an exhalation and a harmony to which the words are little more than the wood and gut of a violin are to the music drawn from the instrument.

§ 2

In *Elia* Lamb is complete master of his instrument. It is necessary to say this emphatically, lest it should be thought that in permitting himself the use of a device which has here been likened to a stammer, he was evading the usual difficulties which confront a writer of prose. No more than a cursory glance at the essays is required to establish the fact that, when he chose, Lamb could write with a plain straightforwardness, but when he does this he is so much the less remarkable, and when we turn to those pieces of which one thinks instantaneously as soon as the name of Elia is mentioned, it is invariably to find that he is using those masterly artifices which depend upon the skilled employment of parenthesis. The extent of his acquired mastery of sentence-structure according to his own perfected individual pattern, is the extent of the difference between the opening page of *Rosamund Gray* and those sentences in *Dream Children* (and elsewhere in *Elia*) which run to a matter of several hundred words between one full stop and the next. The opening of *Rosamund Gray* is in an irritatingly staccato manner: "It was noontide. The sun was very hot. . . . They two lived together. They had once known better days. . . . Our tale hath grief enough in it." No doubt it could be said that this manner of writing is accordant with the simplicity of the tale itself, though such a claim would hardly bear examination. The suggestion has been made to me, with a show of probability, that these brief sentences may be in themselves the transference to paper of Lamb's speech difficulty; that the young man, then only an apprentice to writing, was endeavouring to correct by a studied brevity those obstacles to fluency of which he is likely to have become less self-consciously aware as the years brought a resolute purpose of utilising his deficiencies to purposive ends. Without labouring too much the mature reliance upon the device of parenthesis, it may none the less be noted that it was not merely in his framing of sentences that he used it, but that it did on occasion become part of the whole design. The most remarkable instance of this is in *Old China*, comment upon which belongs to the next chapter. But the use of the parenthetical method as applied to the design of an essay can also be watched, operating in a slightly different manner, in *Dream Children*. There, actually, it is employed in both ways —as an element in the marshalling of sentences and also as an element in the whole design. A characteristic sentence from this essay will serve as an illustration of the method in operation.

Then I told how good she was to all her grand-children, having us to the great-house in the holydays, where I in particular used to spend many hours by myself, in gazing upon the old busts of the Twelve Caesars, that had been Emperors of Rome, till the old marble heads would seem to live again, or I to be turned into marble with them; how I never could be tired with roaming about that huge mansion, with its vast empty rooms, with their worn out hangings, fluttering tapestry, and carved oaken panels, with the gilding almost rubbed out—sometimes in the spacious old fashioned gardens, which I had almost to myself, unless when now and then a solitary gardening man would cross me—and how the nectarines and peaches hung upon the walls, without my ever offering to pluck them, because they were forbidden fruit, unless now and then—and because I had more pleasure in strolling about among the melancholy-looking yew trees, or the firs, and picking up the red berries, and the fir apples, which were good for nothing but to look at—or in lying about upon the fresh grass, with all the fine garden smells around me—or basking in the orangery, till I could almost fancy myself ripening too along with the oranges and the limes in that grateful warmth—or in watching the dace that darted to and fro in the fish-pond, at the bottom of the garden, with here and there a great sulky pike hanging midway down the water in silent state, as if it mocked at their impertinent friskings,—I had more pleasure in these busy-idle diversions than in all the sweet flavours of peaches, nectarines, oranges, and such like common baits of children.

The special points of interest in this, and in numerous other protracted Elia sentences that could be matched with it, are that although it might seem that the conclusion is to be indefinitely delayed, there is no floundering, no uncertainty, no stagnation. The sentence is always progressing, always marching toward its end. And, furthermore, there is no means other than the one adopted whereby precisely the same effect of a recovered memory could be secured. With greater success than any twentieth-century experimental writer, Lamb does bring into notice the stream of consciousness. In the same essay, as clear a suggestion of design is realised—by the interpolation of parenthetical sentences—as could be had in a stretch of

tapestry by the use of a recurrent visual *motif.* Since
we know them so well and have come to accept them
as an inevitable part of the texture of *Dream Children,*
it is quite impossible for us to estimate the extent to
which this essay would be impoverished if it were
denuded of those asides which are the sign-manual
of happy genius.—"Here Alice put out one of her
dear mother's looks, too tender to be called upbraiding"
. . . "Here John smiled, as much as to say 'That would
be foolish indeed' " . . . "Here little Alice spread her
hands" . . . "Here Alice's little right foot played an
involuntary movement, till, upon my looking grave,
it desisted" . . . "Here John expanded all his eye-
brows and tried to look courageous" . . . "Here
John slyly deposited back upon the plate a bunch of
grapes, which, not unobserved by Alice, he had
meditated dividing with her, and both seemed willing
to relinquish them for the present as irrelevant" . . .
"Here the children fell a-crying, and asked if their
little mourning which they had on was not for uncle
John, and they looked up and prayed me not to go
on about their uncle, but to tell them some stories
about their pretty dead mother." It is not so much
the studied artfulness of this device that is remarkable
as the discretion with which it is used. Employed
once too often, it would have become as tiresome as
the antics of a child playing self-consciously for
admiration. Leaving out of account altogether its
appeal to sentiment—an appeal which could have been
made successfully with clumsier means—there is no
alternative to the conclusion that *Dream Children* is
a piece of perfected art. And we may say again, for
the purpose of showing the exact coincidence between
the artist and his instrument, that if those three-hun-

dred-word sentences were attempted by any other writer, the result would be mere bad prose; not because it is impossible to imitate such writing, but because there cannot be any expectation of securing again a personality and a set of circumstances to which that style would be exquisitely appropriate.

§ 3

Given a theme upon which memory and fancy could play, Lamb was also a master in the evocation of places and persons. He could have written a finer book on London than any existing, and in the few fragments on metropolitan scenes which are scattered through the letters there is enough to make us regret that some of the time expended on casual journalism was not given to a fuller exploration of the vistas opened up whenever he thought of London. The first Elia essay, that on the South Sea House, is more remarkable for the sense of animate being which it imparts to the building than for its rapid portraits of some who passed their days there. They at least departed before a final ignobility had settled upon them, but the House, outlasting the generations of men, sank more and more into an irremediable decrepitude which was the more affecting inasmuch as some faded relics of its former pomp and circumstance lingered about its rooms and passages. There is nothing in the world so pitiful as a building which has fallen upon lean or evil days.

When attempting to assign reasons for the discrepancies of impression apparent in the two essays on *Christ's Hospital*—one by the earlier Lamb, the other by Elia—there is ground for thinking that the difference

may be due in part to the presence in *Elia* of a more
or less definite formula. In the first Christ's Hospital
essay it was made to appear almost as though all
was for the best in the best of all possible schools.
Even after a lapse of years Lamb could hardly go
back altogether upon that record, even if he had so
desired, and he therefore fathers the change of view
upon another, whom we recognise to stand for
Coleridge. But there is in the Elia essay a persistent
self-dramatisation at only one remove from Byronic
melancholy. It is not quite that, because Lamb had
too sharp a sense of humour ever to see himself for
long in the trappings of romantic gloom. Yet there
is, time and again, a delicious being-sorry-for-himself.
Lamb was from beginning to end a man of sentiment—
not a sentimentalist, for that again would imply the
absence of humorous self-criticism. For the purposes
of sentiment in literature regrets can be capitalised
sooner than satisfactions: memory is all the pleasanter
for a tinge of picturesque misery or deprivation. The
essay on *Oxford in the Vacation* displays two aspects of
the Elia formula. *First*, that words and sentences were
used as material out of which a design could be made
to impart something additional to meaning. That
Lamb worked thus on a larger scale has already been
shown in the references to *Dream Children*. A single short
sentence from *Oxford in the Vacation* may serve to show
how he employed words as units of design: "The
enfranchised quill, that has plodded all the morning
among the cart-rucks of figures and ciphers, frisks and
curvets so at its ease over the flowery carpet ground
of a midnight dissertation." This sentence no doubt
means something quite clear. In its setting the reader
may take it in his stride without staying to consider

too closely what it means, though the essay can hardly be read attentively without some lingering over that and many other sentences to admire the pictorial quality which they possess without straying into the region of graphic art. The sentence quoted does admittedly employ words and images which might suggest pictures in another medium—"flowery carpet ground", for example—but one cannot, without imposing upon the image a connotation it will not bear, think either of flowers or the patterning of carpets in this connection any more than one can think of the frisks and curvets of the enfranchised quill as the caperings of an heraldic beast. Lamb's patterns have no existence outside the medium in which he creates them; "the flowery carpet ground of a midnight dissertation" is a something, a nothing, an airiness which has neither local habitation nor name outside the region in which Lamb created and we discover it. *Secondly*, while investigating the Elia formula through *Oxford in the Vacation*, we light upon this: "To such a one as myself, who has been defrauded in his young years of the sweet food of academic institution nowhere is so pleasant, to while away a few idle weeks at, as one or other of the Universities." *One who has been defrauded in his young years.* In such phrases as these Lamb strikes the powerful note of picturesque romantic lamentation, and no one who has once read *Elia* with perception needs to be reminded of how often this note is struck, not with a sympathy-begging insistence, but with the same delicacy and discretion as Elia keeps throughout. Does he not himself say in *New Year's Eve*: "It is my infirmity to look back upon those early days. Do I advance a paradox, when I say that, skipping over the intervention of forty years,

a man may have leave to love *himself*, without the impu-
tation of self-love? . . . God help thee, Elia, how art
thou changed! thou art sophisticated.—I know how
honest, how courageous (for a weakling) it was—
how religious, how imaginative, how hopeful! From
what have I not fallen, if the child I remember was
indeed myself,—and not some dissembling guardian,
presenting a false identity, to give the rule to my
unpractised steps, and regulate the tone of my moral
being! That I am fond of indulging, beyond a hope
of sympathy, in such retrospection, may be the symptom of some sickly idiosyncrasy. Or is it owing to
another cause; simply, that being without wife or
family, I have not learned to project myself enough
out of myself; and having no offspring of my own to
dally with, I turn back upon memory, and adopt my
own early idea, as my heir and favourite?''

The presence of *A Bachelor's Complaint of the Behaviour
of Married People* among the Elia essays provides a
convenient opportunity for comparisons between
Lamb's intermediate and his perfected style. That
essay is a favourite with many readers, but it should
not be difficult even for those who care least about
niceties of style to distinguish the superiority of, say,
A Dissertation upon Roast Pig when the two examples
are considered as works of art. *The Bachelor's Complaint*
is heavy-footed in comparison; it moves with a pedes-
trian formality, whereas the true Elia has the gift
of flight. It would not be beyond the abilities of any
writer of quality to provide a syllabus and a catalogue
of the foibles of his married acquaintance which could
bear comparison with Lamb's. There is, if we judge
it by the standard of the best of the other pieces in the
book, a photographic stiffness of outline which would

be unlikely to hold attention and interest if protracted through the whole series of essays. On turning to *A Dissertation Upon Roast Pig* we are in the presence of a writer who has discovered how to free himself from the hard and fast contrivances of prose, and to exercise his own sure power of weaving words and phrases into a new imaginative creation. The subject is only pork; but what pork it is—such diet as never was on sea or land: "There is no flavour comparable, I will contend, to that of the crisp, tawny, well-watched, not over-roasted, *crackling*, as it is well called—the very teeth are invited to their share of the pleasure at this banquet in overcoming the coy, brittle resistance— with the adhesive oleaginousness—O call it not fat— but an indefinable sweetness growing up to it—the tender blossoming of fat—fat cropped in the bud— taken in the shoot—in the first innocence—the cream and quintessence of the child-pig's yet pure food— the lean, no lean but a kind of animal manna—or, rather, fat and lean (if it must be so) so blended and running into each other, that both together make but one ambrosian result, or common substance." Here is a striking and entirely characteristic instance of that divine stammer which bespeaks the true and only Elia. Topics (whether *Roast Pig* or any other) were not to him topics in our earth-bound sense. He did not write essays on topics; he wrote variations on themes, or even (we might say) composed fugues on words. To speak of "variations" or of "fugues" is in a sense inappropriate, because, as Lamb himself said and we have confirmed from other sources, he had no ear. But just as other men have composed nocturnes and symphonies in paint, so did Elia transpose the musical shapes of words into visual patterns, or even into patterns of what might be considered a much lower order, for what is *A Dissertation Upon Roast Pig* if it is not a *Sonata for the Stomach*?

§ 4

In regard to the character-portraits scattered through the essays, Elia stands somewhere between the old manner and the new. While ostensibly he is looking back to the character-writers of the seventeenth and eighteenth centuries, from Cowley to Addison, he is plainly feeling forward to the greater freedom of the chief Victorian novelists. It was both fortunate and unfortunate that Lamb happened to live in an interim period as far as English prose-forms was concerned. The eighteenth-century periodical essay had reached the limits of its capacity before he was born, and the full amplitude of the novel was only just being realised when he died in 1834. *Pickwick Papers*, which was to carry over the eighteenth-century manner and submerge it, was probably about then occurring to the minds of the publishers who commissioned it, and it is fascinating to speculate as to what would have become of Lamb if he had been born twenty-five years later than he was and had been the close friend of Dickens rather than of Coleridge and Hazlitt. There are traces of what has come to be called the Dickensian quality in one or two of Lamb's portraits—in Sarah Battle, for instance, and in Joseph Paice (*Modern Gallantry*)— though much less of free-booting robustness. To have recourse again to visual terms, Lamb drew with a quill, whereas Dickens used a fully-charged brush; but Lamb secured the lifelike effects of the novelists more than the formal graces of the old essayists.

This can be seen even when he is dealing with an unnamed character, as clearly as when he is drawing James Elia or Bridget. The essay on *The Old and the New Schoolmaster* is a case in point. Treated in the seventeenth- or eighteenth-century manner, the staid gentleman in the Bishopsgate stage-coach would have been fixed as a generalised sketch of "a" Schoolmaster. But Lamb gives us, first, a *particular* portrait, and it needs only that the narrative should be translated into dialogue for it to pass at once into the Dickens category. Much is added that would not have been there if Dickens and not Lamb had met that Schoolmaster, just as much is omitted. We should have been without the learned allusions, and without the extraordinarily sensible reflections upon children as a tribe, as well as upon schoolmasters as a tribe. "Boys are capital fellows in their own way, among their mates; but they are unwholesome companions for grown people. The restraint is felt no less on the one side, than on the other." . . . "I would not be domesticated all my days with a person of very superior capacity to my own. . . . Too frequent doses of original thinking from others, restrain what lesser portion of that faculty you may possess of your own. You get entangled in another man's mind, even as you lose yourself in another man's grounds." (Those last two sentences are as perceptive and as sensible as any written by Lamb.) "Why are we never quite at our ease in the presence of a schoolmaster?—because we are conscious that he is not quite at his ease in ours. He is awkward, and out of place, in the society of his equals. He comes like Gulliver from among his little people, and he cannot fit the stature of his understanding to yours."

Dialogue is so infrequent in Lamb's works that it can be considered as almost non-existent, even in *Rosamund Gray*, where the few instances of its use are strangely tentative and awkward. This diffidence about dialogue was unfortunate, for it imposed a handicap that nothing could surmount, and we may often feel surprise that Lamb did not avail himself of so great an aid. How much we wish he had given us one single instance of aunt Hetty's apt back-answers, when he says (in *My Relations*) : "She was a woman of strong sense, and a shrewd mind—extraordinary at a repartee; one of the few occasions of her breaking silence—else she did not much value wit." And yet, though Elia usually denied himself and denies us the most powerful help to characterization, he compensates brilliantly in other ways. If in relation to aunt Hetty the aural appeal is lacking, other senses are brought into play with clearly revealing effect: "The only secular employment I remember to have seen her engaged in, was, the splitting of French beans, and dropping them into a China basin of fair water. The odour of those tender vegetables to this day comes back upon my sense, redolent of soothing recollections. Certainly it is the most delicate of culinary operations."

The most subtle portrait drawn by Lamb is that of his brother John—James Elia of the essays. As we have seen earlier, John Lamb was one who thought chiefly of his own comfort, and according to Crabb Robinson, who could not a-bear him, he was a noisy boor. But we cannot be confident that Robinson was a reliable witness as to the qualities of his *bête noire*. Charles had been indignant and deeply hurt by John's wish that Mary should be committed permanently to an asylum, yet there is no doubt that he had a strong affection for his elder—there was twelve years difference between them. The excellent skill and cleverness of the description of James Elia cannot fully be appreciated without a fair knowledge of the original as he was in the flesh, for Charles contrived to present the truth with the utmost kindness. Where Crabb Robinson might have said that John was a selfish hog, Elia writes: "With great love for *you*, J. E. hath but a limited sympathy with what you feel or do. He lives in a world of his own, and makes slender guesses at what passes in your mind." What by Crabb Robinson might have been interpreted as blustering cowardice is elevated by Elia to: "He is courageous as Charles of Sweden, upon instinct; chary of his person, upon principle, as a travelling Quaker." Another would perhaps have declared that John was a dull-witted philistine; but his brother refines the limitation: "He has not much respect for that class of feelings which goes by the name of sentimental. He applies the definition of real evil to bodily sufferings exclusively—and rejecteth all others as imaginary." At no moment in the essay can it be said that Lamb is merely glossing over John's deficiencies or varnishing him for the public eye. Every one of John's evident weaknesses is there, but touched in with a superb tact and sensibility, and a delicate but none the less biting humour.

CHAPTER TWELVE

THE LAST ESSAYS OF ELIA

§ I

CREDIT must be given to America for having extended to *Elia* in volume form the favour with which the essays had been received in transit by the readers of the *London Magazine*. Journalism, often derided as a disreputable poor relation of literature, can claim Charles Lamb as its own child, for such fame as he knew in his lifetime depended almost entirely upon his contributions to a periodical with a circulation which would nowadays be considered negligible. But while the collected *Elia* was neglected by bookbuyers in England (Lamb did not live to see a second edition) the Americans liked the book so well that they pirated a further collection five years before *The Last Essays of Elia* came out in London in 1833. This, too, failed to interest English bookbuyers and Lamb was destined to go to his grave a neglected author. Speculation is frequently busy around the question of whether a sequel is or is not as good as its original. Of course, *The Last Essays of Elia* is not in the ordinary sense a sequel; both books embody a not very regular series. Nevertheless, it would not have been surprising to find some sign of flagging in the pen of Elia, considering that six years separated the first essays in *Elia* from the final Popular Fallacy in the *Last Essays*. Not all the pieces are equally attractive to the present-day reader and perhaps not all of them are marked by the ineluctable charm that is universally credited to their author; but, at least, no one would hesitate to grant that in Popular Fallacies XIV and XV (*That We Should Rise with the Lark* and *That We Should Lie Down with the Lamb*) the characteristic spirit of Elia is retained; and in a competition for naming the best of all the essays it is certain that a number of those in the second volume would be chosen. If he did other things as good, it is indisputable that Lamb never did anything better than *Old China*. That essay represents the perfection of the Elia technique. The whole of the magnificent central portion is a sustained parenthesis, to which the brief remainder serves as a frame—the frame being as perfect as what it frames. The several references to Mary Lamb (Bridget) in *Elia* are completed by the tale of her reminiscent talk in *Old China*. Mere familiarity may make us unaware of the literary and human riches compressed into its half-dozen pages. Altogether apart from the verbal re-creation of the old blue willow-pattern china, which lives in Lamb's phrases as it never could have done in the clay and glaze and colour of its own material being, there is the whole character of Mary Lamb expressed in her long monologue upon the consolations of (relative) poverty. We know her less by what Charles and others told descriptively of her elsewhere than by what is revealed of her here as she speaks. And though this is not in the usual sense dialogue, it is an earnest of the effects Lamb might have obtained if he had been less chary of permitting his characters to use their own voices.

Meditations upon poverty account for some of the best writing in the *Last Essays*; poverty comparative and poverty absolute. Lamb is, most part of the time, more interested in poor *persons* than in the horror of poverty itself, but there is no sentimental romanticising of it. When Bridget tends toward that view of their own straitened days he reminds her that there is much to be said for the comfort of a balanced domestic budget at each year's end. The psychological effects of poverty—or, perhaps we should say, of shabby or decayed gentility—have seldom been more devastatingly shown than in *Poor Relations*. Lamb himself may have been chiefly sensible of the effects upon himself of the shifts and subterfuges and the clumsily-veiled obsequious-insolence of these unfortunates, but he also lays bare to the reader the vileness of a state in which the victim, though poor, must make pretence of keeping a hold upon some less despised condition. Mr. Lucas has reminded readers of Lamb of two instances in which he drew what might be taken as a forecast or first sketch of Micawber. One is the character of Bigod in *The Two Races of Man* in *Elia*; the other, Captain Jackson in the *Last Essays*. At those points where we feel a special need of enlightenment, the ample information about Lamb breaks down, and there is no means of knowing whether Captain Jackson is an imaginative creation or the characterisation of an actual person. He has the ring of authenticity, and there is no reason for supposing that Lamb kept in reserve any such developed power of fictionalising as would be necessary for drawing the Captain from the void. Under the cover of humour, it is an affecting picture that Elia gives of Jackson, subsisting with his wife and daughters upon the most frugal fare, yet

P

making-believe in the presence of visitors that his table offers choice viands and wine, with silver to boot. And so full-bodied was the make-believe that Lamb could write: "Wine we had none; . . . but the sensation of wine was there. . . . Shut your eyes, and you would swear a capacious bowl of punch was foaming in the centre, with beams of generous Port or Madeira radiating to it from each of the table corners. You got flustered, without knowing whence; tipsy upon words; and reeled under the potency of his unperforming Bacchanalian encouragements."

In the appreciation of Lamb written directly after his death, P. G. Patmore in the *Court Magazine* gave special praise to an essay on *The Children of the Poor*. This, no doubt, was number XII in the Popular Fallacies series, *That Home is Home though it is never so homely*. The repudiation of certain widely-current opinions—or pretences, as he was inclined to believe them—gave Lamb peculiar satisfaction. The majority are dismissed lightly or with ingenuity, but number XII is tackled in a different spirit. It is not customary to think of Lamb as taking a close personal interest in what we call social questions, and one would not in a general way number him among the pamphleteers or writers of tracts. His *Confessions of a Drunkard*, cast in a mould of dark sincerity, has been used by teetotal advocates for their own purposes, but as a piece of advocacy it has less force than *That Home is Home though it is never so homely*, which might very well be reprinted as a leaflet for use today by those who work on behalf of slum-dwellers. Lamb begins by drawing a comparative picture of the poor man's home and the ale-house, that more cheerful-seeming image of a home to which he often resorts. Contrary to the suppositions of prosperous people, the poor man (Elia avers) has no cheerful wife and clean contented family. Cheerfulness and other desirable domestic qualities have been effaced by misery;—and the poverty-beset wife's face, "is that a face to stay at home with? is it more a woman, or a wild cat? alas! it is the face of the wife of his youth, that once smiled upon him. It can smile no longer. What comforts can it share? what burthens can it lighten? Oh, 'tis a fine thing to talk of the humble meal shared together! But what if there be no bread in the cupboard? The innocent prattle of his children takes out the sting of a man's poverty. But the children of the very poor do not prattle. It is none of the least frightful features in that condition, that there is no childishness in its dwellings. Poor people, said a sensible old nurse to us once, do not bring up their children; they drag them up. The little careless darling of the wealthier nursery, in their hovel is transformed betimes into a premature reflecting person. . . . A child exists not for the poor as any object of dalliance; it is only another mouth to be fed, a pair of little hands to be betimes inured to labour. . . . The children of the very poor have no young times. It makes the very heart to bleed to overhear the casual street-talk between a poor woman and her little girl, a woman of the better sort of poor, in a condition rather above the squalid beings which we have been contemplating. It is not of toys, of nursery books, of summer holidays (fitting that age); of the promised sight, or play; of praised sufficiency at school. It is of mangling and clear-starching, of the price of coals, or of potatoes. The questions of the child, that should be the very outpourings of curiosity in idleness, are marked with forecast and melancholy providence.

It has come to be a woman before it was a child. It has learned to go to market; it chaffers, it haggles, it envies, it murmurs; it is knowing, acute, sharpened; it never prattles. Had we not reason to say, that the home of the very poor is no home?" Very rarely did Elia exchange urbanity for such furious indignation, but he did it once before in the *Last Essays* when complaining against the two-shilling admission charge to Westminster Abbey—in *The Tombs in the Abbey*, an essay which originally formed part of the open *Letter to Southey* containing Lamb's reply to the Poet Laureate's charge of an insufficiency of religious feeling in *Elia*.

§ 2

Certain remarks in the *Sanity of True Genius* might tempt one to recant the opinion that Charles Lamb was not a sound critic of poetry, but there is no real ground for conceding more than that, in his last years, he may have approached a recognition that what he hitherto asked of poetry was inadequate to the nature of poetry, since he had stressed its reproductive and imitative aspect more than its creative power. That essay, moreover, leaves room to doubt whether Lamb's assurance was not too sure when he lays it down as "impossible for the mind to conceive of a mad Shakespeare". In so far as a poet comprises within himself all those states of being he establishes in poetry, it is not only possible for us to conceive of a mad Shakespeare, but necessary also. Either Lear's state is that of madness, or it is a colourable imitation of madness foisted upon him from outside by a person who knew nothing of the matter; if the latter is true, then Lear's madness is no more than a literary fake. And surely to say this would be silly. Shakespeare, like every great poet, was one who apprehended and drew into himself—or discovered already within himself—every experience native to the people in his plays. He did not "imagine" these states and experiences, merely; he *was* them. Lamb says the poet "is not possessed by his subject, but has dominion over it". That is a half-truth; no more. The poet has dominion over what he is possessed by. A man cannot by taking thought or by sending his imagination on an excursion create a Lear or a Hamlet. It is necessary for the poet to *become* Lear or Hamlet, while at the same time remaining his master and master of himself. Anyone can "imagine" a mad person, or a man distraught; a minor writer can both imagine and transfer that image to paper; but no one becomes a Shakespeare so. The great poet does not imagine or contemplate the experience, nor look at it from outside: he and the experience become one. Lamb asserts that the poet "ascends the empyrean heaven, and is not intoxicated". These are the terms of a romantic criticism which tends itself to become intoxicated; and there is nothing much to be said against the statement if it means no more than that a poet does not need to go out and get drunk with a mænad in order to write a poem about a bacchic revel. But if it is trying to be literally true under the cover of romantic language, then as a view of poetry it is utterly false. Of course the poet who ascends the empyrean heaven is intoxicated—with the glory of the heaven, if glory is what he finds there. Otherwise, what is he doing in heaven? Is he only a reporter to come back and describe what he saw there? Or is he not under an impulsion to give us (in such degree as we are capable of receiving it) his own empyrean experience? If Lamb had said that the poet ascends the empyrean heaven and is not instantaneously consumed to annihilation when he looks upon the divine countenance, there would be something in it. Further, it is not true that "poetic talent . . . manifests in the admirable balance of all the faculties,"—unless Lamb meant (and he certainly did not) to distinguish poetic talent as an inferior stage to poetic greatness. Poetic genius manifests itself in a totality of the faculties; the word "balance", and the image it suggests of a grocer-like ouncing of this and that until the beam is levelled, is inappropriate; and, anyhow, if it were true, why not a proportionate manifestation of the faculty of madness? But madness, says Lamb, "is the disproportionate straining or excess" of any one of the usual "sane" faculties. Not always, surely. Is there not a species of divine possession, not unknown among great poets, which passes under the name of madness? Is not every variation from the common standard in any particular time designated madness? The poet is both sane and insane. He differs from the ordinary in being able to manipulate his madness exactly as much as he is manipulated by it. If we may recur to Lamb's figure, it is not that the poet does not become intoxicated but that he gets thoroughly intoxicated without losing his head or the use of his feet. To say that "he is not possessed by his subject but has dominion over it" implies all too easily that the poet, with raised forefinger, says to his subject, "Down, good Fido!"—though it would be sounder to suggest that he opens his arms to his subject with "Hail, bright spirit" and submits to its embrace. He is intoxicated, but (unless he is a bad poet and therefore no poet at all) he is not debauched. In spite of such sharp differences of view as to the nature of the poet, there are sentences in the *Sanity of True Genius* which suggest that Lamb was coming to realise, or had realised theoretically all along, that poetry has an existence in its own right: "From beyond the scope of Nature if he summon possible existences, he subjugates them to the law of her consistency"—though it might be remarked, concerning this sentence, that while, in *Lear*, Shakespeare summons possible existences from beyond the scope of Nature, he does not appear to subjugate them to her laws; rather does he appear to postulate laws, that we can only guess at, equally beyond her scope.

§ 3

The character-sketch of the supposedly defunct Elia with which Lamb prefaced the *Last Essays* contains enough of the truth for us to take it, with suitable reservations, as a final close-up of a person who was, we cannot doubt, not only a singular character but a more contradictory one than James Elia was accounted by his brother to be. There has never been much need to whitewash Lamb—except perhaps to quieten the testy who cannot tolerate horse-play and to humour the prudish who are certain that drink, tobacco and snuff should be nowhere outside the devil's locker. According to himself, Lamb-Elia was both liked and bitterly hated; he gave rein to his tongue without always calculating the consequences; he was so detached in regard to religion that some set him down as a free-thinker, others as a bigot; he was addicted to irony and jest; he was neither orator himself, nor encouraged oratory in others. In person small and ordinary (so the account runs) he selected his friends with a preference for idiosyncrasy more than for accomplishment. We have grown accustomed to thinking of him as almost continuously deferential and considerate of others' feelings, but in fact he was sometimes "remonstrated with for not making concessions to the feelings of good people" and "would retort by asking, what one point did these good people ever concede to him?" "He had a horror, which he carried to a foible, of ever looking like anything important and parochial. He thought that he approached nearer to that stamp daily. He had a general aversion from being treated like a grave or respectable character, and kept a wary eye upon the advances of age that should so entitle him. He herded always, while it was possible, with people younger than himself. He did not conform to the march of time, but was dragged along in the procession. His manners lagged behind his years. He was too much of the boy-man. The *toga virilis* never sate gracefully on his shoulders. The impressions of infancy had burnt into him, and he resented the impertinence of manhood. These were weaknesses; but such as they were, they are a key to explicate some of his writings."

EPILOGUE

THE OLD ARMS OF HUMANITY

A REVIEWER in the *London Magazine* (January 1820) speculating as to the identity of Barry Cornwall,[1] who had recently issued a collection of poems, wrote, after suggesting several improbable names: "Nor is Mr. Cornwall Mr. Lamb. We have heard it said he is. If so we are blockheads. It appears to us that he has much of Mr. Lamb's feeling, and love of simplicity, and pathos, and familiarity with the gentle and sorrowful things of the world; but he has not Mr. Lamb's imagination or depth, nor has he quite so extensive a sympathy with humanity. He wants the 'something far more deeply interfused', which we find in Mr. Lamb's pieces." To this catalogue of qualities should be added two remarks by other contemporaries. Crabb Robinson noted that Lamb "reasons from feelings"; and Leigh Hunt, in an obituary notice in the *London Journal*, wrote that his friend "was only at his ease in the old arms of humanity". While it has been no small part of my purpose in the foregoing pages to claim that Charles Lamb had another and darker side to his temperament and outlook, his wide popularity has unquestionably depended upon the

[1] The pen-name of B. W. Procter, who afterwards wrote one of the earliest books on Charles Lamb.

characteristics which seemed uppermost to the witnesses here quoted. He settled genius on the hearth,
and as genius is a wild thing it is rare to find it established in so homely a situation. Possibly if the hearthrug
had not been Mary Lamb's customary habitation,
Charles' genius would have wandered afield or have
been dissipated in the wake of other pursuits. We
cannot tell. But we can say with assurance that the
hearth no more crippled or limited Lamb's genius
than the peculiar conditions of the Elizabethan theatre
limited Shakespeare's. Genius will out—when it is
genius; it does not demand to be coddled and pam-
pered. More genius has been dulled by petting than
has been destroyed by penury, and the genius of
Elia broke through the restrictive domestic confines
of one who was, in the main, "something in the City".
When Lamb secured more favourable circumstances
for the production of literature, genius forsook him.
The hearth is, ideally, the congenial source of those
features enumerated by the *London Magazine* critic
as the distinguishing marks of Lamb's writings: feeling,
simplicity, pathos, familiarity and sympathy with gentle
and sorrowful things. The hearth, too, belongs to those
who "reason from feelings". It is just these characteristics, and especially the last, that causes the modern
intellectualist to depreciate the high value set upon
Lamb twenty to thirty years ago. To reason from
feelings does not conduce to the hard clarity of thought
now in vogue in a narrow corner; it is a process that
encourages, rather, a warm clamminess of the mental
integument inimical to straight thinking. But, with
whatever reluctance, we must accept as a foregone
conclusion for our time, if not for all time, that
humanity at large will do as Lamb did in these

matters. Perhaps by the ordinance of God the great majority of human creatures put emotion before thought, impulse before logic. We may go further and say that something outside ourselves puts emotion and impulse first. No doubt it is desirable that these springs of action should be brought under the control of the intellect, though we should concede that point with hesitation and doubt. It has yet to be satisfactorily demonstrated that a dictatorship of the mind is less tyrannical or less pernicious than a dictatorship of the emotions. Popularity cannot help but flow where feeling is strongest, and we should rather rejoice that the general sentiment is perceptive enough to find good in Lamb than deplore its inability to fathom profounder authors—if, in truth, there are any more profound, in a right interpretation of the word. Intellectual fashions change from year to year, and those who have lived long enough to see the advance-guard of yesterday become the back numbers of today, are sceptically unmoved by the hectorings of self-conscious learning. It happens, at this moment, that among a vocal few the heart is out of fashion. We might ask *Why?*—since the heart is the indispensable member of the personal commonwealth of organs and faculties. It is out of fashion only among those who feel no certainty of their own power to control the unpredictable activities of the heart. We can say to the brain, "Do thus and thus" and in due time it is done. We say to the heart, "Do thus"—and the heart does its own will, in despite of us. A rare few in human experience have been successful in establishing a harmonious working relationship between brain and heart, and of these Lamb was one. In him and his work the heart ruled, yet only as the first among equals—

disciplined and directed and touched to issues that do not cease to be fine because they belong to the common stock of man's experience. When empires and civilisations are broken and universities levelled beneath the grass, the remnants of humanity must start again where Lamb begins and ends—at the hearth, which is, in the final resort, the cradle of wisdom as well as of sentiment.

CHRONOLOGY

1764   (December 3) Mary Lamb born

1775   (February 10) Charles Lamb born at 2 Inner Temple Lane

1780   Sees his first play (*Artaxerxes* at Drury Lane)

1782   Enters Christ's Hospital
      Meets Coleridge there

1789   Earliest known writings
      Leaves Christ's Hospital

1790   Works in Joseph Paice's office, Bread Street Hill

1791   Begins work at South Sea House

1792   Leaves South Sea House
      The family leaves the Temple and goes to Little Queen Street, Holborn
      Charles enters office of East India House

1794   Evenings with Coleridge at the *Salutation and Cat* in Newgate Street
      End of his love romance with Alice W—— [Ann Simmons]

1795   Spends six weeks in madhouse at Hoxton

1796   (September 22) Mary in a fit of insanity kills her mother and is placed in a private asylum
      The family moves to Chapel Street, Pentonville

1797   Aunt Hetty dies
      Mary moved from asylum to lodgings at Hackney
      Charles meets the Wordsworths at Nether Stowey
      Begins *John Woodvil* and *Rosamund Gray*

1798   Writes *The Old Familiar Faces*
      Rosamund Gray published

1799   Father (John Lamb) dies

1801   Charles and Mary living at Mitre Court Buildings, Temple
      Charles writes for *The Albion*

1802 *John Woodvil* printed
1803 Writes *Hester*
1805 First of his children's books
1806 *Mr. H.* produced at Drury Lane
1807 *Tales from Shakespeare* published
1808 *Dramatic Specimens* published
     Adventures of Ulysses
1809 *Mrs. Leicester's School*
     Leaves Mitre Court for Southampton Buildings,
       Holborn, and thence to 4 Inner Temple Lane
     Poetry for Children
1810 Contributes to *The Reflector*
1815 Visits Mackery End
1816 Stays at Dalston
1817 Moves to Great Russell Street, Covent Garden
1818 *The Works of Charles Lamb* (in 2 volumes) published
1820 First meeting with Emma Isola, afterwards adopted
       by Charles and Mary
     Begins contributions under Elia pseudonym in
       London Magazine
1821 John Lamb (brother) dies
1822 Visits France
1823 *Elia* published
     Moves to Colebrook Cottage, Islington
1825 Retires from East India House on pension
     The Pawnbroker's Daughter
1827 *The Wife's Trial*
     Moves to Enfield
1830 *Album Verses* published
     Lodging in London while Mary is under restraint
1833 *Last Essays of Elia* published
     Moves to Edmonton
     Emma Isola marries Edward Moxon
1834 (July 25) Death of Coleridge
     (December 22) Charles falls and injures his face
     (December 27) Death of Charles Lamb
1847 (May 20) Death of Mary Lamb

BIBLIOGRAPHY

THE EDITIONS OF LAMB'S WORKS INCLUDED IN THIS LIST
ARE ONLY THOSE WHICH CONTAIN BIOGRAPHICAL OR
CRITICAL MATTER BY THE SEVERAL EDITORS

1835   *Charles Lamb: His Character*, by E.M. [Edward Moxon]

1837   *The Letters of Charles Lamb*, with a sketch of his life (2 vols.), by T. N. Talfourd

1848   *Final Memorials of Charles Lamb*, including letters not previously published, with sketches of some of Charles Lamb's friends (2 vols.), by T. N. Talfourd

1855   *My Friends and Acquaintances* (3 vols.), by P. G. Patmore

1866   *Charles Lamb*, by B. W. Procter (Barry Cornwall)

      Miscellanies, by A. C. Swinburne

      Charles Lamb: His friends, his haunts and his books, by Percy Fitzgerald

1868   *Complete Correspondence and Works of Charles Lamb*, with an essay on his life and genius by G. A. Sala (1 vol. only published)

1869   *Diary, Reminiscences and Correspondence of Henry Crabb Robinson* (2 vols.), selected and edited by T. Sadler

1870   *Complete Correspondence and Works of Charles Lamb*, with an essay on his life and genius by T. Purnell assisted by Emma Isola

1874   *Mary and Charles Lamb: Poems, Letters and Remains*, with reminiscences and notes, by W. C. Hazlitt

1878   *Recollections of Writers*, by Charles Cowden Clarke and Mary Cowden Clarke

1882   *Charles Lamb*, a biography, by Canon Alfred Ainger (English Men of Letters Series)

1883   *Mary Lamb*, by Mrs. A. Gilchrist (Eminent Women Series)

1887   *Obiter Dicta* (Second Series), by Augustine Birrell

1889   *Appreciations*, by Walter Pater

1893   *Bernard Barton and his friends*, by E. V. Lucas

1897   *The Lambs: Their lives, their friends and their correspondence*, by W. C. Hazlitt

1898   *Charles Lamb and the Lloyds*, by E. V. Lucas

1899–1900 *Life and Works of Charles Lamb*, with introduction and notes, by Canon Alfred Ainger

1900   *Lamb and Hazlitt*, by W. C. Hazlitt
        (New York) *Charles Lamb, or Elia*, by G. E. Woodberry

1903   *Sidelights on Charles Lamb*, by Bertram Dobell

1903–5 *Works of Charles and Mary Lamb* (7 vols.), edited by E. V. Lucas

1905   *The Life of Charles Lamb* (2 vols.), by E. V. Lucas

1922   *Blake, Coleridge, Wordsworth, Lamb, etc.*, being selections from the remains of Henry Crabb Robinson, edited by Edith J. Morley

1925   *Cambridge and Charles Lamb*, by G. E. Wherry

1927   *Recollections of Charles Lamb*, by George Daniel

        The Correspondence of Henry Crabb Robinson with the Wordsworth Circle, 1808–66, edited by Edith J. Morley

1932   *Lamb before Elia*, by F. V. Morley

1933   *Charles Lamb and his Contemporaries*, by Edmund Blunden

INDEX

Actors, 21, 91, 102–3, 103, 129, 130

Adventures of Ulysses, The, 132, 169–70

Albion, The, 123

Album Verses, 133–4, 146

Alice W——, 44–6, 49, 90, 122

Allsops, The, 74

Amicus Redivivus, 64

Ancient Mariner, The, 59

Anna (*see* Alice W——)

Austen, Jane, 158

Bachelor's Complaint of the Behaviour of Married People, A, 185, 201

Baldwin, Cradock and Joy, 134

Ballad: Noting the Difference of Rich and Poor, A, 145

Barbara S——, 91

Barbican, 39

Barnet, 186–7

Barrenness of the Imaginative Faculty in the Productions of Modern Art, 100

Barton, Bernard, 73

Beaumont and Fletcher, 44, 97, 165, 172

Belshazzar's Feast, 101

Benger, Elizabeth Ogilvie, 83

Bigod, Ralph (John Fenwick), 209

Bird, William, 27, 28

Blakesware, 23, 25, 46, 187

Blank Verse, 122

Blue-coat School (*see* Christ's Hospital)

Boyer, Rev. James, 31, 32, 121

Bridget Elia (*see* Mary Lamb)

Brighton, 109, 110

British Museum, 112

Browne, Sir Thomas, 98 178, 179, 180, 191

Burney, Martin, 73

Burton, Robert, 98, 179, 180

Cambridge, 76, 94, 109, 110

Captain Jackson, 209–10

Carlyle, Thomas, 11, 81, 115

Champion, The, 126

Chapel Street, Pentonville, 50, 76, 90

Chapman, George, 174

Chapter on Ears, A, 185, 186

Children of the Poor, The, 210–12

Chimney Sweepers, *The Praise of*, 72

China, Old (*see* Old China)

Christ's Hospital, 28 ff., 38, 62, 72, 121, 181, 198–9

Christ's Hospital Five-and-Thirty Years Ago, 28, 34, 198

Christ's Hospital, Recollections of, 28, 198

Clairmont, Mrs. (Mrs. William Godwin), 68

Clarke, Charles Cowden, and Mrs. Mary, 85, 86, 88

Clifford's Inn, 63

Cockney School, The, 65 ff.

Colebrook Row, Islington, 65, 76, 87

Coleridge, Samuel Taylor, 3, 4, 5, 28 ff., 46, 48, 49, 50, 51, 56–61, 65, 77–8, 82–3, 98, 122, 140, 141, 199, 203

Compleat Angler, The, 97, 179

Q

Composed at Midnight, 144
Confessions of a Drunkard, 19, 184–5, 210
Confessions of H. F. V. Delamore, Esq., 185–7
Congreve, William, 104
Cornwall, Barry (*see* B. W. Procter)
Court Magazine, 74, 210
Covent Garden, 44, 76, 84, 108
Crown Office Row, Temple, 21, 40

Dalston, 17, 76
Defoe, Daniel, 97, 184, 187, 191
De Quincey, Thomas, 42–3
Dickens, Charles, 18, 190, 203–4, 209
Dissertation on Roast Pig, A, 201–3
Dobell, Bertram, 185
Dodd, James, 103
Dramatic Specimens, 132–3, 165, 171 ff.
Dream Children, 2, 9, 45, 194–8, 199
Drury Lane Theatre, 83, 102, 129–30, 154, 179
Dyer, George, 62 ff., 78, 90, 115, 169

Eastbourne, 110
East India House, 40 ff., 51, 70, 111–12, 123, 183
Edax on Appetite, 181
Edmonton, 76, 116, 146
Elia (origin of the pseudonym), 135
Elia, 12, 58, 65, 98, 126, 133, 137, 138, 139, 158, 178, 185, 190 ff., 207, 208, 209, 212
Elia, Last Essays of, 74, 133, 184, 207 ff.
Elliston, R. W., 129, 130
Enfield, 70, 76, 88, 112, 113, 115, 116
Essex Street Chapel, 23

Examiner, The, 126, 127–8
Excursion, The, 60–1
Falstaff's Letters, 72

Fenwick, John (*see* Ralph Bigod)
Field, Mary (Grandmother Field), 22, 23–5, 38, 49
Field, Rev. Matthew, 31
Fielde, Francis, 102
Fielding, Henry, 97
First Going to Church, 167–8
Fleet Street, 27, 86, 107, 108
Foxe's *Book of Martyrs*, 22
Fulham, 115
Fuller, Thomas, 176–7

Garrick, David, 21
Gentle Giantess, The, 110
Gentleman's Magazine, 126
Gipsy's Malison, The, 134, 147–50
Gladmans, The, 24, 38
Godwin, Mary Wollstonecraft, 68
Godwin, William, 66, 67–8, 105, 130–2
Godwin, Mrs. William (formerly Mrs. Clairmont), 68, 130–2
Goldsmith, Oliver, 26
Good Clerk, The, 126, 183–4
Great Russell Street, Covent Garden, 76, 84

Hackney, 17, 49
Hardy, Thomas, 162–4
Hastings, 82, 109, 110
Hazlitt, Sarah, 67, 77, 83
Hazlitt, William, 2, 66, 89, 121, 129, 203
Hazlitt, Mrs. William (*see* Sarah Hazlitt)
Hester, 90, 142–3
Hetty, Aunt (*see* Sarah Lamb)
Hogarth, William, 96, 99–101
Hogarth, On the Character and Genius of, 99–101
Hood, Thomas, 66, 115, 144, 147

Hospita, 181
Hoxton, 17, 52, 78
Hunt, John, 125, 128
Hunt, Leigh, 66, 67, 75, 121, 125–8, 217
Hypochondriacus, 143

India House (*see* East India House)
Indicator, The, 126
Inner Temple Lane, 76, 99
Innocence, 144
Islington, 17, 49, 65, 87, 112
Isola, Emma, 87, 94–5

John Woodvil, 128, 150–2
Johnson, Samuel, 27
Julie de Roubigné, 160

Keats, John, 66, 141, 175
Kelly, Fanny, 91 ff.
King and Queen of Hearts, The, 131

Lamb, Elizabeth (Charles' mother), 20, 21–2, 40, 47, 49
Lamb, Charles: his personality, 1 ff., 54–5, 74–5, 79, 215–6; his emotional discipline, 3, 9; his preference for obscurity, 4; his way with philosophers, 5; his domestic tragedy, 6, 47 ff.; his place in literature, 10 ff., 121; his stammer, 13; and the art of writing, 13–14, 59, 136; his London, 17–18; his habits, 19–20, 79 ff., 94; his relatives, 20 ff., 38, 46 ff., 51, 66, 102, 205–6, 208; his birthplace, 21; in Hertfordshire, 22, 23 ff., 44 ff., 87, 99, 187; his early reading, 22, 36; his childish fears, 22; ministrations of Aunt Hetty to, 23, 29; and Coleridge, 29, 46, 48, 49, 50 ff., 56 ff., 65; has smallpox, 23; is lame, 23; anecdote of his childhood, 26;

early schooling, 26 ff.; his handwriting and spelling, 27; at Christ's Hospital, 28 ff., 38, 72; his debt to Samuel Salt, 28, 38, 71; and to Timothy Yeats, 28, 38; and to Joseph Paice, 38–9; at the New River, 29, 65; becomes a Deputy Grecian, 32; his literary style, 34, 45, 136, 190 ff.; in the Temple, 21 ff., 35 ff., 54 ff., 76, 99; in Paice's office, 38; at South Sea House, 38 ff., 46; and the *London Magazine*, 39, 123, 128, 134 ff., 184–7, 217, 218; moves to Holborn, 40, 47; at East India House, 40 ff., 51, 111; as bookman, 44, 96 ff., 188–9; his early love-affair, 44 ff.; and Mary's insanity, 6, 47 ff., 52, 77 ff., 115–16; moves to Pentonville, 50; and religion, 50, 137, 215; his many friends, 54 ff., 61, 65 ff., 89, 115, 188; at the *Salutation and Cat*, 57; dislikes the epithet "gentle," 57; his insanity, 58; and Southey, 58, 65, 212; and Wordsworth, 59 ff., 65; and Manning, 60, 73, 112; and Crabb Robinson, 61, 68 ff., 80; his evening parties, 61, 88–9; and George Dyer, 61 ff., 115; at Islington, 65, 76, 87; and *The Reflector*, 67, 125–6, 182–3; his life with Mary, 76 ff., 116; Carlyle's opinion of, 81; his opinion of intellectual women, 82–3; his farce, *Mr. H.*, 83, 128 ff., 152 ff., 182; moves to Covent Garden, 84; his personal appearance, 86, 89; indifferent to Nature, 86, 106–7; his garden, 87; his love of walking, 87; his adopted daughter, 87, 94–5,

134; and animals, 87; and Hester Savory, 90; and Fanny Kelly, 91–4; as poet, 90, 122, 139 ff.; and the theatre, 93, 102 ff., 128 ff., 150 ff.; and pictures, 96, 99 ff.; and Thomas Westwood, 97, 113–14, 136–7; on Hogarth, 99 ff.; on Restoration comedy, 104–5; love of London, 107 ff.; at the seaside, 109–10; an amateur of letters, 111; retires on pension, 111; at the British Museum, 112; moves to Enfield, 112; his horror of moving, 112–13; moves to Edmonton, 116; his accident and death, 117; as journalist, 123 ff.; his *Rosamund Gray*, 122, 158 ff., 194–5, 205; his earlier essays, 126; satirizes the Prince Regent, 127–8; as dramatist, 128 ff., 150 ff.; his children's books, 131–2, 165 ff.; as critic, 132–3, 171 ff., 212 ff.; his *Works* (1818), 133, 176 ff.; his *Album Verses*, 133–4; his dejection, 137–8; his uncollected essays, 182 ff.; his misadventure at Barnet, 186–7; his *Essays of Elia*, 190 ff.; his *Last Essays of Elia*, 207 ff.; his homely genius, 218–20

Lamb, John (Charles' father), 20, 21, 25, 28, 40, 46, 51, 52

Lamb, John, the younger (Charles' brother), 20, 39, 46–7, 49, 66, 135, 136, 140, 204, 205–6, 215

Lamb, Mary: in relation to Charles and his work, 7, 26, 28, 38, 44, 45, 76 ff., 86, 96, 98, 102, 123, 138, 184, 209, 218; in Hertfordshire, 20, 22, 23–5; in the Temple, 22, 54–6, 96; her early reading, 36; her dressmaking business, 46–7; she kills her mother during a fit of insanity, 47 ff.; her insanity recurs, 52, 78, 113, 115, 184; placed under restraint, 49, 52, 78, 113, 138; and her brother John, 49, 205; returns to live with Charles, 52; her friendship with Sarah Stoddart (Mrs. Hazlitt), 67, 77; and Crabb Robinson, 69–71; her disposition, 78–9; her appearance, 84–6; as authoress, 82 ff., 131 ff., 164, 166, 169, 170, 176; her female friends, 82–3; wishes to die first, 86; and Fanny Kelly, 93; and Emma Isola, 94–5; her reading, 97; and Charles' books, 98; at the theatre, 102, 129; and Thomas Westwood, 114; her rambling talk, 116, 208; and the Godwins, 131 ff., 169

Lamb, Sarah (Aunt Hetty), 22–3, 29, 38, 47, 49, 181, 205

Landor, Walter Savage, 115

Last Peach, The, 187–8

Leadenhall Street, 41, 112

Le Grice, Charles Valentine, 34, 35

Lepus Papers, The, 198

Letter of Elia to Robert Southey, 58

Lincoln's Inn, 36

Little Queen Street, Holborn, 40, 47–8, 50, 76

Lloyd, Charles, 72–3, 122

Lloyd, Robert, 73

London (Lamb's praises of), 59, 106 ff., 178

London Journal, 217

London Magazine, 39, 123, 126, 128, 134 ff., 184–7, 217, 218

Lovel (*see* John Lamb, Charles' father)

Lucas, E. V., 46, 87, 98, 124, 188, 209

Lyrical Ballads, 59, 60

Mackenzie, Henry, 160
Mackery End, 24
Manning, Thomas, 42, 60, 63, 73, 90, 107, 112
Man of Feeling, The, 160
Many Friends, 188
Margate, 109
Marlowe, Christopher, 165, 172–3
Martin, John, 101
Mille Viae Mortis, 122
Milton, John, 56, 60, 143
Mr. H., 83, 128 ff., 152–4, 182–3
Mrs. Leicester's School, 24, 132, 166 ff.
Mitre Court Buildings, Temple, 55, 76
Modern Gallantry, 38
Morning Chronicle, 47–8
Morning Post, 123, 124
Moxon, Edward, 73, 95
Munden, Joseph, 102–3
My Relations, 47, 205

Newgate Street, 28, 29, 34, 56, 181
New River, 29, 65, 87
New Times, The, 126, 188
New Year's Eve, 200–1
Newspapers Thirty-five Years Ago, 123
North, Christopher, 115
Notes and Queries, 114, 117, 137

Odyssey, 169
Old Benchers of the Inner Temple, The, 52
Old China, 2, 195, 208
Old Familiar Faces, 122, 143
Old Margate Hoy, The, 110
On an Infant Dying as Soon as Born, 134, 147
On Burial Societies, 180
On the Artificial Comedy of the Last Century, 104–5
On the Character and Genius of Hogarth, 99–101

On the Conversation of Authors, 89
On the Custom of Hissing at the Theatres, 126, 182–3
On the Danger of Confounding Moral with Personal Deformity, 126
On the Inconveniences Resulting from Being Hanged, 126, 181
On the Tragedies of Shakespeare, 174
Oxford, 76, 109, 110
Oxford in the Vacation, 64, 65, 110, 199–200

Paice, Joseph, 38, 203
Pantisocracy, 58
Patmore, P. G., 74–5, 80, 81, 210
Pawnbroker's Daughter, The, 150, 154–5
Pentonville, 50, 76, 90
Philanthropist, The, 126
Plumers, The, 23
Poems, Lamb's, 45, 46, 139 ff.
Poetical Pieces on Several Occasions, 21
Poetry for Children, 132, 170–1
Poor Relations, 209
Pope, Alexander, 109
Popular Fallacies, 208, 210–12
Prince Dorus, 132
Procter, B. W. (Barry Cornwall), 52, 53, 89, 217
Proust, Marcel, 14, 136

Quarterly Review, 60–1, 126

Readers Against the Grain, 188–9
Recollections of Christ's Hospital, 28, 198
Reflections in the Pillory, 186–7
Reflector, The, 67, 125, 126, 178
Reynold's Mrs. (Lamb's school-mistress), 26, 28, 44
Rickman, John, 68
Robinson, Henry Crabb, 43, 61, 69 ff., 79, 80, 89, 92, 96, 97, 110, 115, 129, 205, 206, 218

Rosamund Gray, 122, 158 ff., 194
Ruskin, 193

Salt, Samuel, 21, 28, 36, 40, 46, 71
Salutation and Cat, 56–7
Sanity of True Genius, 212–15
Savory, Hester, 90, 91
Scott, John, 134
Sea Voyage, The, 167, 168–9
Shacklewell, 17
Shakespeare, 3, 56, 60, 79, 83, 103, 131–2, 148, 151, 164 ff., 169, 172–5, 180, 212–15, 218
Shaw, Bernard, 91
She is Going, 145–6
Shelley, 141
Siddons, Mrs., 122
Sidelights on Charles Lamb, 185
Simmons, Ann (Alice W——), 44–6, 49, 90
South Sea House, 38 ff., 46, 135–6, 193, 198
Southampton Buildings, Holborn, 76, 115
Southey, Robert, 58, 59, 65, 106, 137, 212
Specimens of English Dramatic Poets Who Lived about the Time of Shakespeare, 132–3, 171 ff.
Stevenson, Robert Louis, 7, 11
Stitch, Wilhelmina, 8
Stoddart, Sarah (*see* Sarah Hazlitt)
Strand, The, 107, 108
Superannuated Man, The, 2, 112

Tales from Shakespeare, 83, 131–2, 164 ff., 169
Talfourd, T. N., 26, 34, 89, 117
Taylor and Hessey, 134
Taylor, John, 134, 135
Temple, The, 21, 28, 29, 34, 35 ff., 55, 71, 84, 96, 181

Tennyson, 140, 142
Terry, Ellen, 91
Tess of the D'Urbervilles, 162
That Home is Home though it is Never so Homely, 210–12
That We should Lie Down with the Lamb, 208
That We should Rise with the Lark, 208
This Lime-tree Bower my Prison, 57
Times, The, 68–9
Tombs in the Abbey, The, 212
Two Races of Men, The, 98, 209
Ulysses, The Adventures of, 132, 169–70

Wales, Prince of (Prince Regent, afterwards George IV), 67, 127–8
Walton, Izaak, 97, 98, 178
Westminster Abbey, 212
Westwood, Thomas, 97, 113–14, 116–17, 136–7
Westwood, Mrs. Thomas, 113–14
Westwoods, The, 113, 115–16
Whale, The Triumph of the, 127
White, James, 72
Widford, 87
Wife's Trial, The, 150, 152, 156–7
Wilcox, Ella Wheeler, 3
Witch Aunt, The, 167, 168
Witches, and other Night Fears, 167
Wollstonecraft, Mary, 68
Woolman, John, 73
Wordsworth, Dorothy, 7, 84, 110
Wordsworth, William, 3, 4, 7, 42, 58, 59, 65, 70, 106 ff., 140
Works of Charles Lamb, The (1818), 133, 176 ff.
Worthing, 110
Wycherley, William, 104

Yeats, Timothy, 28, 37